Don't Let Them PSYCH YOU OUT!

George Zgourides, Psy.D.

D0148762

Loompanics Unlimited
Port Townsend, Washington

The material in this book is in no way meant to be a substitute for medical, psychological, legal, or other professional advice or services. This book is sold for information purposes only. Neither the author nor the publisher will be held accountable for the use or misuse of the information contained in this book.

Published by:
Loompanics Unlimited
PO Box 1197
Port Townsend, WA 98368
Loompanics Unlimited is a division of Loompanics Enterprises, Inc.

ISBN 1-55950-097-2
Library of Congress Catalog Card Number 93-77857

Dedication

To all the souls out there who absolutely, positively,
and without a doubt *dread* interpersonal conflicts.

And to three couples who by their example continue to inspire me:

Ricks and Terri Warren
and
Tim and Deb Storlie
and
Mark Tilson and Francine Florendo

Acknowledgments

Putting a book together requires a great deal of time and effort on the part of many people. I especially wish to thank Michael Hoy, Steve O'Keefe, and the folks at Loompanics Unlimited for helping to make ***Don't Let Them Psych You Out!*** a reality. I also wish to thank my parents, Ted and Katherine Zgourides, for their manuscript ideas, and Lou Rollins for his editorial assistance.

About the Author

George Zgourides, Psy.D. is a licensed psychologist (Texas) and an Assistant Professor of Psychology at the University of Portland (Oregon), with academic interests in human sexuality, anxiety, cognitive therapies, and Christian rational living. Besides authoring some 20 professional articles, Dr. Zgourides is co-author, with Ricks Warren, Ph.D., of *Anxiety Disorders: A Rational-Emotive Perspective* (1991, Pergamon Press/Allyn and Bacon), and author of the forthcoming book, *Perspectives in Human Sexuality* (HarperCollins Publishers). During summers, Dr. Zgourides practices as a clinical psychologist near San Antonio, Texas. During the rest of the year, he is a consultant with Associated Counselors in Vancouver, Washington. In his spare time, Dr. Zgourides enjoys jogging, composing music, and playing his electric bass guitar.

Contents

INTRODUCTION

Everybody's had to deal with them — difficult people. From the nosy neighbor and meddling relative to the overbearing boss and pushy salesman. Our society is literally full of people trying to get an upper hand by manipulating and "psyching out" the meek and innocent. And there's usually one or more of these folks in every crowd, regardless of where you live, work, worship, travel, or socialize.

So if you want to preserve your sanity, maintain your personal integrity, and avoid getting psyched out, *Don't Let Them Psych You Out!* has a lot to offer you. To survive the brutality of everyday life, I believe it is essential that you take charge of yourself — your thoughts, emotions, and reactions to others — something I refer to as *psychological self-defense*. In other words, armed with the right cognitive, emotional, and behavioral ("cognitive-emotional-behavioral," or CEB) weapons, a person need not be bullied by *anybody*, including the unscrupulous, manipulating types. You're not really *required* to do what "they" say. You don't *need* to worry about "their" opinions. You don't *have* to stand by and let "them" walk all over you. Much like the martial artist who develops various skills to protect himself physically, you can develop skills to protect yourself psychologically. Yes, there's great personal power in knowing who you are and what you can choose to do (or more importantly, *not* do) in any situation.

Unfortunately, most of us like to play it safe, believe and do what we're told, and find every imaginable way to avoid conflicts. The sad fact is: *most people would rather back down than stand their ground or fight back!* While perhaps convenient in the short run, this philosophy of retreating in the face of conflict isn't a very effective or healthy way to embrace life. In fact, it creates a vicious cycle of backing down, feeling bad, backing down again, feeling worse, etc., until the person feels out of control emotionally. Sure, it's uncomfortable facing fears and standing up for yourself, but in the long run it's the best way to avoid chronic unhappiness and even serious emotional problems. Every person has the right to make his own decisions and be his own person without someone else invading his personal or psychological space. "The System" (not to mention "Big Brother"!) does enough of this anyway — who needs it from bosses and relatives, too?

My purpose, then, in writing *Don't Let Them Psych You Out!* is to help all the "nice" people out there who are fed up with feeling stomped on. This is not to say there's some magic answer that will make all the bad things in life go away. To the contrary, not everyone is going to live happily ever after — something the typical psychologist may not tell you. (It's not good for business!) Most people will face many disappointments and disillusionments. Life is hard. Not everything can always be fixed. And not everyone can quit work, assume a new identity, and hit the road.

There are effective CEB strategies, however, that you can use to minimize the emotional pain and stresses of daily living. For example, the person who can't change or leave a particular situation (e.g., a stressful job) can learn to "rethink" his situation, assert himself, and verbally handle whatever problems and annoyances arise. In *Don't Let Them Psych You Out!*, I'll describe many such strategies to help you better cope with and even overcome some of life's hardest blows — simple, proven strategies that can be applied to all interpersonal conflicts.

In all truth, I originally began developing *Don't Let Them Psych You Out!* for my own use. As a psychology professor and clinical psychologist, my expected role in society is that of someone who really has it together. While true in many areas of my life, I've always had trouble when "caught off guard" by intimidating, controlling, and pushy people. Like many shy and reserved folks, I'm easily startled when challenged or faced with confrontations. I go blank, worry about losing face, shuffle around for a quick comeback (which never works), and later feel bad about not having had it together. I mean, my reputation as a psychologist and decent person is at stake, right? Well, as it turns out, not really, but during a confrontation it can seem that way. So after years of dealing with difficult bosses, clients, and students, I decided there had to be a better way. And I found it.

First, I realized that *there is the potential for conflict in every encounter*, and that, just like a good Boy Scout, I need to always be alert and prepared for whatever problems might just happen along in the course of my day. Second, I found that *altering my interpretations of events* in my life is what really makes a difference, not necessarily trying to change the events themselves. Today, I still encounter assorted problems at work, school and home, but now I'm better prepared to handle them by keeping a rational, realistic attitude about it all. For example, it's not really *terrible* if my students dislike my classes, only *inconvenient* in some cases, and *no problem at all* in most cases. Third, I found that I could best verbally counter difficult people by *preparing myself ahead of time with "lines" I can spout off without having to think, i.e., specific responses I'd memorized and practiced* to give me something intelligent to say when challenged, allow me time to gather my senses and think my way out, and defuse an uncomfortable situation.

Here's a brief example to illustrate my last point. People tend to think of me as an open-minded, nice guy, so they are always calling and asking me for favors. For example, one of the most common requests I get is to give free talks at generally inconvenient times, like after work or on Saturday mornings. Unfortunately, I usually get caught off guard, go blank, and then agree to do something I don't really want to do. After deciding to regain control of my schedule, I prepared the following READY REPLIES (RRs) for unreasonable requests and demands on my time:

"I already have plans."

"I have very little free time these days."

"My calender is completely booked."
"Let me think about it."

With these sorts of vague, "canned" replies, I have ready-made statements that give me an out, or at least more time to think about the request. Simple, but effective! (Yes, I've gotten out of giving a lot of free talks this way!) And I've practiced these RRs so much that they're now automatic, which leads me to my final point...

I realized that *practicing my newfound skills is the best way to keep them.* As I've continued to rehearse and practice these strategies over the years, I've become much more at peace with myself and comfortable being assertive with difficult people. I've also found these methods to be helpful for the many students and clients I've taught and counseled (at least the ones who really want to make changes in their lives).

Don't Let Them Psych You Out! is an alternative psychology self-help book, devoted to helping you develop mental and verbal weapons for handling everyday confrontations and preventing others from getting the psychological edge on you. Specifically, *Don't Let Them Psych You Out!* is based on modern CEB principles and methods, which have witnessed an amazing increase in use in the field of psychology over the last thirty years. This cognitive-behavioral "revolution" (a la Drs. Albert Ellis, Aaron Beck, and Donald Meichenbaum) has primarily been concerned with explaining how one's thoughts, interpretations, and perceptions of events influence one's feelings, behaviors, and basic manner of acting in the world, as well as how to apply the principles of effective change and coping to everyday life. Thus, *Don't Let Them Psych You Out!* differs from other books on the market in its application of the newest in scientific self-help methods to practical psychological self-defense.

Don't Let Them Psych You Out! divides into three basic parts. In *Part I*, "The Basics of Psychological Self-Defense," I'll show you how to use psychological self-defense to regain control of your life. In *Part II*, "When You Psych Yourself Out," I'll help you apply the information presented in the first chapters to personally troublesome emotions, such as fear and anger. And in *Part III*, "When Others Psych You Out," I'll show you how to use psychological self-defense to protect yourself from the mental and verbal attacks of others, such as relatives, bosses, and salespeople.

But it doesn't stop there! In *Don't Let Them Psych You Out!*, I'll also show you how to relax and center yourself before going into potentially difficult situations; how to reflect and paraphrase what someone else is saying; various ways to say NO; how to ward off unwelcome, malicious criticism; and much more. These are the same techniques I teach to my students, trainees, and clients — here for you in written form, and at a fraction of the cost of seeing me (or any other psychologist) at the office. What a deal!

Finally, although mass market pop psychology books are everywhere, you've probably noticed that these tend to be unrealistically positive and wordy. Not so with *Don't Let Them Psych You Out!* You see, I'm a "meat and potatoes" guy, and I really believe in keeping it simple and getting to "the point" as quickly as possible. To this end, I've purposely kept the chapters of *Don't Let Them Psych You Out!* concise and readable. In my experience, self-help readers generally prefer materials that are straightforward, easy to understand, and readily applicable.

I don't want to imply, however, that everything on the pop psychology market is bad. To the contrary, there are some really good books available, and I believe several of them deserve a quick mention. (It's important for you to read as many quality self-help psychology books as possible to get the most out of the techniques presented in this book.) A few of the better pop psychology books are Eric Berne's *Games People Play*; Robert Bramson's *Coping With Difficult People*; Jay Carter's *Nasty People*; Wayne Dyer's *Your Erroneous Zones*; Suzette Haden Elgin's *The Gentle Art of Verbal Self-Defense*; Albert Ellis and Robert Harper's *A New Guide to Rational Living*; Maxwell Maltz's *Psycho-Cybernetics*; Manuel Smith's *When I Say No, I Feel Guilty*; Nicholas Capaldi's *The Art of Deception*; Joan Menninger and Eleanor Dugan's *Make Your Mind Work For You*; and Victor Salupo's *The BS Syndrome*. For your convenience, I've included a list of "Selected References" at the end of this book that I think you'll find helpful in your search for mental and emotional freedom.

Today, you stand at one of those junctures in life. Are you willing to open yourself to a new way of thinking? Can you accept the possibility that there's a different, better way? Will you take my challenge to learn a more effective way of handling yourself and other people? I believe that by choosing to read this book, you've already answered YES to these questions. So congratulations! You've taken that all-important first step — you've decided to take charge of yourself and your life! I sincerely hope the information presented in the following pages will help you accomplish just that.

A Brief Word of Caution

After considerable thought I decided to preface this book with a brief caution. Why? Because the techniques, strategies, and methods described in *Don't Let Them Psych You Out!* are very, very powerful. They aren't to be taken lightly. If used properly, psychological self-defense techniques can bring about positive changes in your life. But if used improperly or maliciously, they can cause mental and emotional harm to others.

Why am I so concerned about how you use psychological self-defense? The answer is simple. I could never endorse your doing something that goes against my values. I'm a "born-again" Christian (and make no apologies for it). I firmly believe in turning the other cheek, giving someone your coat as well as your shirt, and forgiving and praying for your enemies. These are values dear to my heart. To suggest that you use psychological self-defense to hurt others purposely and without provocation would be hypocritical on my part. My motive in writing *Don't Let Them Psych You Out!* is not to harm, but to provide readers with practical pointers for dealing with difficult people and situations.

In closing, whatever your personal religious beliefs, please remember the cosmic principle, "What goes around comes around." In other words, if you intentionally sow the seeds of pain and suffering among your fellow human beings, that's exactly what you'll reap in return.

Part I
The Basics of Psychological
Self-Defense

Chapter 1
Can I Really Regain
Control Of My Life?

Have the courage to act now. You can always quit later.
— **George Zgourides**

The following is an excerpt from my client David's journal:

"How would I describe my life? I feel like I'm running on a treadmill, with someone else controlling the speed lever. It's like I'm going as fast as I can, but everybody wants me to go faster. And no matter what I do, nothing is ever right or enough. For some reason, I'm supposed to do more and give more — you know, 110 percent. I get dumped on all day at work. I go home and get dumped on by family and neighbors. Then I go to church and get dumped on there. When's it all going to stop? I'm getting sick and tired of the whole thing." (David, age 41; from the Author's files)

Or as my friend Mike recently wrote to me:

"I hate the rat race of big-city American materialism. It costs me half of everything I earn just to wake up in the morning. Around every corner there's someone waiting to exploit me (sounds a little paranoid, huh?). I really hate the idea of getting some office job shuffling papers, juggling numbers, and counting beans with only a couple of weeks vacation a year until I die; while someone else who has no respect for me makes 10 times my salary from all the work I do." (Mike, age 30; Author's files)

I can't begin to tell you how many people I've talked to over the years who feel like my client David and friend Mike. I've been there myself on many occasions. Often life just seems out of check. Someone else is at your switchboard. If it's not the mortgage company, tax man, or ladies auxiliary at church wanting a chunk of your derriere, it's your boss, co-workers, spouse, relatives, or neighbors. You give and give and give until there's nothing left. In exchange, you end up feeling burned out, exhausted, and resentful. What a way to spend the few short years you have in this world!

Here are some more of the kinds of comments that I regularly hear from clients, students, and friends:

"I get tongue-tied when somebody asks me to do something I don't want to do. I usually end up giving in instead of turning them down."
"It really hurts my feelings when my family criticizes me."
"At work I feel like a dancing dog who has to perform for his supper!"
"Why can't my neighbors just mind their own business?"
"I'm tired of jumping through someone else's hoops."
"I hate to shop. I can get talked into buying everything I don't need."
"Everyone keeps trying to tell me who I'm supposed to be and what I'm supposed to do."
"I'm so busy taking care of everyone else's sh** that I feel like a one-legged man in an a**-kicking contest."
"I've lost control of my life."

I'm sure at least a few of these statements hit pretty close to home for you. If so, you probably feel as if you're doomed to live according to what I and others call the "Big Lie" — those societal myths that say you're *supposed* to do what you're told, you *must* make other people happy, you *should* never disagree or challenge the establishment, you *need* to keep up with the Joneses, and you *have* to step out of the way when others push you aside. These are all-too-familiar beliefs for many people in our culture.

Fortunately, I have some good news for you. You don't have to buy the "Big Lie." You can use your inborn *free will* to make your own decisions and be your own person. *Your life is not out of your control; you've simply chosen for some reason to relinquish control to others!* That's right. You've let go of your life and placed it in the hands of people who are happy to take over for you.

It doesn't happen all at once. It's an insidious process. Give a little here. Lose a little there. Let someone step on you just this one last time. People like to control you. They want to tell you what to do. They like the power you give them. Unfortunately, you lose a little more of yourself each time you let others psych you out — which is just fine with the people who want to run your life.

"You mean I've done all of this to myself?" For the most part, yes. In all truth, you're probably your own worst enemy! But there's a positive side to this deal. Just as you relinquished control, *you can reclaim control of your life at any time.* Yes, you can take it back without having to give it a second thought. Why? Because it's yours — and always has been.

At this point, you may be asking yourself, "Why do I let people do this sort of thing to me? Why am I so quick to hand over my keys? How do I get myself into these kinds of messes?" Although I can't specifically answer these questions for you, given your unique background and circumstances, I can certainly offer you some clues to help you find your own answers.

Some of your problems may rest with your basic personality style. For example, if you try to make people like you, yet feel continually imposed upon and exploited, you may have what psychologists refer to as an *amiable* personality type. The typical amiable is friendly, likes to maintain warm relations with others, does his or her best to avoid disagreements, and gives in to others' demands. As a result the amiable often holds a subordinate position at work, and is the one everyone asks for favors.

In contrast to this is the *driver* personality type. The typical driver is demanding, couldn't care less about warm relations, relishes the chance to disagree and win arguments, and rarely compromises or gives in. As a result, the driver is often a CEO, director, manager, or supervisor at work, and is never asked for favors.

Putting an amiable and a driver together produces an instant power imbalance, which can easily turn into an exploitable situation if the amiable isn't careful. The driver will instinctively try to dictate the amiable's thoughts and moves, which the amiable will allow for the sake of "keeping the peace" (though he or she may not be happy at all about giving in). People usually exhibit varying degrees of these two (and other) personality styles, although most have a dominant tendency one way or the other.

I want to be clear here that having either of these personalities isn't inherently good or bad. As a society we really need both types of people. For example, the best managers in the world tend to be drivers. In other words, what I'm *not saying* is that all drivers are mean controlling types, and that all amiables are weak "yes" types. What I *am saying,* however, is that exploitive, unscrupulous, and manipulative people tend to be drivers, while meek, humble, and agreeable people tend to be amiables.

Another psychology theory that may help explain why you let people take advantage of you is *attribution theory.* Simply stated, this theory holds that people attribute their life circumstances and problems to either "external" factors (e.g., other people; the weather) or "internal" ones (e.g., temperament; mood). The more external your perspective, the more you feel like a victim of life circumstances. The more internal your perspective, the more you feel in control of life circumstances. So which type of person do you think is the most susceptible to others' influence and persuasion? You've got it — the externalizer. The key to using attribution theory to regain control of your life is to acknowledge the importance of *reattributing* your life problems to internal causes rather than external ones.

You'll notice throughout *Don't Let Them Psych You Out!* that I affectionately refer to the difficult people you encounter in everyday life as your *opponents,* rather than as your enemies, assailants, foes, or the like. I use the term "opponent" because there's no implication that the other person is inherently bad or evil. (For example, consider how the term "opponent" is used in competitive sports.) Granted, some of your daily opponents may seem like evil incarnate (e.g., your boss or supervisor), while others may be the people closest to your heart (e.g., your spouse and family). Nasty or nice — they can all be opponents for whom the same basic psychological self-defense methods apply.

Have you ever heard the saying, "The best defense is a good offense"? Well, nothing could be truer when it comes to reclaiming your life. And that's where *Don't Let Them Psych You Out!* comes in. By learning and applying the techniques presented herein, you take charge of yourself by playing an active offense, so to speak. You're prepared for whatever darts are thrown at you. You can handle whatever nasty comments come your way. You're ready to say NO!!! to whatever unreasonable requests and demands are directed at you. Yes, you can be your own person — content and confident in your ability to handle and protect yourself in virtually every situation.

Don't get me wrong, though. None of this is easy to do. In fact, it's quite hard for most people to change deeply-embedded patterns (thinking or otherwise). But with time and effort, as well as strong motivation on your part, it can be done.

If you don't take charge of your life, someone else will!

And that's my golden message of the day. Remember, only *you* have the power to regain control of your life. Only *you* can do something about situations you don't like and people who get on your nerves. Only *you* can make it all happen.

Chapter 2
How Thoughts and Emotions Cause Problems

Men are disturbed not by things, but by the views they take of them.

— **Epictetus**

Central to the psychology behind **Don't Let Them Psych You Out!** is the famous quote above, attributed to the 1st Century A.D. Greek philosopher, Epictetus. According to the Greek and Roman Stoics, it's not the world that causes you problems, rather it's how you look at the world. Even William Shakespeare wrote of this in *Hamlet,* "For there is nothing either good or bad but thinking makes it so." In other words, your emotional problems are caused, not by "externals" such as your boss, kids, or the weather, but by how you see and evaluate these things.

As an example of the power thinking has on emotions and behavior, consider the following two scenarios. In the first, Jack is walking down the street and sees a man looking out an apartment window. The man sees Jack and begins to shout, scream, and call him every possible four-letter word in the book. This, of course, angers Jack, who screams back and throws something at the man. In the second scenario, Jack is walking down the street and sees a man looking out a window at a local mental hospital. The man sees Jack and begins to shout, scream, etc. This time, however, Jack feels sorry for the man, pays him little attention, and continues on about his business. See how this works? In both of these scenarios, the bottom line event is the same — a man screaming expletives at Jack. But Jack's *interpretations* of these events differ, and so do his *reactions*.

Let's look specifically at *how* thinking affects aspects of yourself and life. In the following diagram, we see that life events, beliefs, and reactions all interact and influence one another. Of particular note is the direct influence that beliefs have on feelings and behaviors.

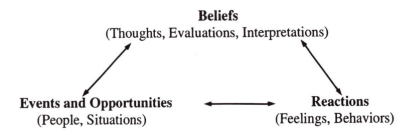

Beliefs
(Thoughts, Evaluations, Interpretations)

Events and Opportunities   **Reactions**
(People, Situations)   (Feelings, Behaviors)

According to this "Event-Belief-Reaction" model, it's your evaluations and interpretations of people and situations that prompt you to feel and act the way you do. And it's your reactions that largely determine what sort of opportunities (if any) will become available. For example, the guy who continually believes and tells himself he can't get a date, gets depressed about it, berates himself, and acts like a real drag inadvertently causes others to shy away from him and refuse his invitations for dates. The more he's turned down, the more he believes and tells himself he can't get a date, gets depressed about it, etc. — all of this serving to reinforce and perpetuate a vicious cycle of negativity.

Okay, I've made my point — life events, thinking, and reacting all influence one another. But what about "emotional problems"? What *types* of thinking patterns create mental and emotional disturbances for the average person?

Almost all of life's upsets and emotional problems come from *demanding* rather than *preferring* types of thinking. People who feel anxious, angry, or guilty don't just *prefer* or *desire* something, they also *demand, dictate,* and *require* that they get what they want. For example, a person might *demand* that everyone approve of, love, and accept him in all respects, thus *generating his own anxiety* when he fails to attain these things. Or he might *dictate* that others treat him thoughtfully or fairly, *becoming hostile or angry* when they don't. Finally, he might *require* that everything in life be pleasurable and trouble-free, *browbeating himself* when the going gets rough.

Most of the time when a person experiences an upset of one sort or another, he's telling himself that something out there is *terrible* or *awful* rather than merely *disadvantageous* or *inconvenient.* Many cognitive psychologists term this process *catastrophizing, disasterizing, terriblelizing,* or *awfulizing.* For example, the catastrophizer might *conclude* that he is a *terrible* person because he's imperfect. Or he might *insist* that the world is an *awful* place when others don't treat him the way he wants.

Whenever a person catastrophizes — i.e., believes something in life (e.g., not getting along with a classmate) is *horrible* or *disastrous* rather than merely *unpleasant* or *unfortunate* — he's subscribing to any of a number of false assumptions, such as:

- The situation is totally bad, even worse than bad.
- The situation makes me utterly miserable.
- I can't tolerate the situation one minute longer.
- The situation shouldn't exist because I don't like it.
- I must find a perfect solution to and fix the situation, or else I'm a failure and a rotten person.

Erroneous hypotheses like these, which can't even be proved or disproved, become personal devils — the kind you create for yourself and allow to rule your life. And as you religiously accept and believe in them, they *will* bring about fear, depression, guilt, shame, anger, and feelings of helplessness and worthlessness in virtually everything you do.

People engage in many types of nonsensical thinking. Following are 13 of the worst offenders, collected from the writings of various cognitive-behavioral experts (e.g., Drs. Ellis, Beck, Burns, Dryden, and DiGiuseppe; also reviewed in Warren & Zgourides, 1991, pp. 14-15):

1. *Mental filtering:* Focusing on specific details at the expense of other important aspects of a situation.
2. *Mind reading (fortune telling):* Presuming to know what others think, feel, or plan to do.
3. *All-or-nothing thinking:* Seeing everything in "black-or-white" terms.
4. *Overgeneralizing:* Using words like *always* and *never;* applying the characteristics of one member to its entire group.
5. *Minimizing (downplaying the positive):* De-emphasizing one's positive characteristics and accomplishments.
6. *Magnifying (upplaying the negative; catastrophizing):* Overstating the negative aspects of a situation.
7. *Jumping to conclusions:* Drawing conclusions about people and events without the necessary evidence.
8. *Accusing:* Blaming others without the necessary evidence.
9. *Emotional reasoning:* Assuming one's emotional state reflects the way things really are.
10. *Personalizing:* Blaming oneself for some negative event.
11. *I-Can't-Take-It-Another-Minute-itis (low frustration tolerance):* Easily becoming frustrated when wants aren't met.
12. *Damnation (negativizing):* Being excessively critical of self, others, and the world.
13. *Perfectionism:* Requiring that everyone and everything in the universe be flawless and without blemish.

These and other types of distorted thinking generally lead to various beliefs and assumptions that people use to drive themselves crazy. I fondly refer to these nonsensical beliefs as *Crazy-Makers* (CMs). (Distorted beliefs are also termed *Irrational Beliefs* (IBs), *Cognitive Distortions*, *Negative Automatic Thoughts*, and *Negative Self-Talk*, depending on the author.) CMs seem logical and well-founded, but are in fact untruths (partial or complete) based on opinions and misconceptions rather than the way things truly are. Following are 11 of the most common CMs or Irrational Beliefs, according to Dr.

Albert Ellis in his book, *Reason and Emotion in Psychotherapy* (1962; pp. 61-88):

1. The idea that it is a dire necessity for an adult human being to be loved or approved by virtually every significant other person in his community.
2. The idea that one should be thoroughly competent, adequate, and achieving in all possible respects if one is to consider oneself worthwhile.
3. The idea that certain people are bad, wicked, or villainous and that they should be severely blamed and punished for their villainy.
4. The idea that it is awful and catastrophic when things are not the way one would very much like them to be.
5. The idea that human unhappiness is externally caused and that people have little or no ability to control their sorrows and disturbances.
6. The idea that if something is or may be dangerous or fearsome one should be terribly concerned about it and should keep dwelling on the possibility of its occurring.
7. The idea that it is easier to avoid than to face certain life difficulties and self-responsibilities.
8. The idea that one should be dependent on others and needs someone stronger than oneself on whom to rely.
9. The idea that one's past history is an all-important determiner of one's present behavior and that because something once strongly affected one's life, it should indefinitely have a similar effect.
10. The idea that one should become quite upset over other people's problems and disturbances.
11. The idea that there is invariably a right, precise, and perfect solution to human problems and that it is catastrophic if this perfect solution is not found.

More recently, Dr. Ellis (Ellis, 1988, p. 60) condensed all of this information into a "*must*urbatory ideology," proposing that all IBs arise from three basic, absolutistic *musts:*

MUST #1: I *must* perform well and/or win the approval of important people, or else I am an inadequate person! (Demands about self.)

MUST #2: You *must* treat me fairly and considerately and not unduly frustrate me, or else you are a rotten individual! (Demands about others.)

MUST #3: My life conditions *must* give me the things I want and have to have in order to keep me from harm, or else life is unbearable and I can't be happy at all! (Demands about the world.)

CMs can also take the form of various *Cognitive Blocks*, or specific irrational notions that interfere with healthy living. Cognitive Blocks often begin with such words and phrases as, "I can't...!" "What if...?" "Oh no...!" or "How awful...!" For example, here are some typical CBs people have about sex:

- I can't do that! What would so-and-so think?
- What if I can't keep my erection this time?
- Oh no, what an embarrassing view of my privates!
- How awful of me to sound like a rutting hog during sex!

Any of this sound familiar to you? It should. Human beings have a biological vulnerability to faulty thinking. And if you're honest about it, at this very moment you could probably list at least a few CMs of your very own. (But, by all means, don't get down on yourself for having CMs! Crooked thinking is just another aspect of being human.) In upcoming chapters, I'll have much more to say about CMs and how they are responsible for a wide variety of everyday problems.

Having identified some of the primary causes of mental distress and emotional bondage, let's now turn our attention to the particulars of *reframing* life's difficulties.

Chapter 3
Rethinking
Away Your Problems

Change your thoughts and you change your world.
— **Norman Vincent Peale**

We learned in the last chapter that a great deal of human unhappiness stems from faulty modes of thinking and believing. In other words, we saw that *people drive themselves crazy!* Life's tough and gives you lots of lemons. There's no doubt about it. But you're the one who ultimately decides whether or not you're going to make lemonade or squeeze lemon juice in your eyes.

So what's the solution to negative, irrational, unrealistic, distorted, crooked, disturbed, and faulty thinking? Cast out the devils! Yes, exorcise them! But how?

First, you accept the fact that you're a *fallible human being.* By embracing your humanity, you set the stage for overcoming your mental upsets.

Second, you stop *demanding* and *complaining* about not getting what you want. You get rid of all those *shoulds, musts, haves, oughts,* and *needs.* Only then can you adopt a more realistic and rational attitude — one of *preferring* and *accepting.*

Next, you remove the *terribleness* and *horribleness* from those things in life that bother you, instead acknowledging the fact that nothing in the entire universe is anything other than *unfortunate* and *inconvenient.*

Finally, you realize that although pain, problems, and conflicts are a part of life, you need not bow to them or let them tear away at you. Instead, you can rethink those seemingly noxious stimuli, seeing them for what they really are — opportunities for personal growth, not defeat! You may be stuck, for example, in a difficult situation (e.g., living next door to irritating neighbors). If you can't or don't want to leave or move, and you've exhausted all other possibilities, you can use your head to cope. Beautiful, isn't it? The answer is right there between your ears. Again, "Men are disturbed not by things, but by the views they take of them." *You can tolerate virtually anything if you'll take control of your thinking!* This entire process of identifying, challenging, and eliminating Crazy-Makers (CMs) is known in psychology as *cognitive reframing,* or *cognitive restructuring.*

And now for some specifics. Cognitive reframing involves several important steps. The first step is becoming familiar with the types of CMs people regularly use (as detailed in the last chapter), and then identifying the ones that *you* use in any given situation ("SIT," or *trigger*). Consider this example:

SIT: A friend passed me by on the street without looking at me or saying hello.
CMs: Nobody likes me anymore. I'm a *failure,* and that's *terrible.*

Here we see how an individual comes up with a CM in response to a normal, everyday sort of occurrence. The SIT in this case, like most SITs, is a *neutral* event. That is, there's no implication of thought or intention on the part of the friend. He or she may have been preoccupied with how to pay their taxes or where to eat lunch, and thus wasn't paying attention to who was on the street. It's only after jumping to conclusions and negativizing that the other person perceives the SIT as a negative event. The person falsely concludes that, "Because my friend didn't say hello, nobody likes me." The person also takes it one irrational step further when concluding that, "I'm a failure because nobody likes me, and that's terrible." See how these leaps of illogic work? Here's another example:

SIT: The salesman isn't smiling.
CMs: I *must* make people happy. I'd better buy his what-cha-ma-call-it so he'll be happy.

Again, we have a neutral SIT, but a distorted perception. The faulty line of reasoning here is, "The salesman isn't happy because he's not smiling. I must be doing something wrong to make him not be happy. Since I'm supposed to make everybody around me happy, I'd better do something to make him happy. I know, I'll buy his product. Then he'll be happy, approve of me, and I'll feel like a good person." Crazy, isn't it? Yet people think and act like this all the time.

The second step in the reframing process involves coming up with *disputes* for, or challenging, your CMs. Disputes often begin something like this:

- What proof do I have that...?
- Who says...?
- Where's the rule that says...?
- Who cares if...?
- What's the worst thing that would happen if...?
- What's the probability that...?
- Why do I need to...?
- So what if...?

Let's dispute our two examples:

SIT: A friend passed me on the street without looking at me or saying hello.
CMs: Nobody likes me anymore. I'm a *failure,* and that's *terrible.*
Disputes: What proof do I have that nobody likes me? What's the probability that nobody likes me? Why must I think of myself as a failure if nobody likes me? What's the worst thing that would happen even if I were a failure?

and

SIT: The salesman isn't smiling.

CMs: I *must* make people happy. I'd better buy his what-cha-ma-call-it so he'll be happy.

Disputes: Who says I must make people happy? Who cares if the salesman is happy or likes me? Where's the rule that requires me to buy something I don't want to make someone happy? Anyway, what assurance do I have that the salesman would be happy even if I did buy his product? Why worry about it?

The third step in the reframing process is devising one or more *Sensible Replies* (SRs) to replace your original CMs. Basically, this involves answering your Disputes. SRs to the above CMs might go something like this:

CMs: Nobody likes me anymore. I'm a *failure,* and that's *terrible.*

SRs: I have no proof that people dislike me. In fact, there's very little chance of this being true. Even if they did, even if they *absolutely hated* me and I was an *incompetent failure,* it'd only be inconvenient, not terrible. What others think of me has nothing to do with my worth as a person.

and

CMs: I *must* make people happy. I'd better buy his what-cha-ma-call-it so he'll be happy.

SRs: I'm responsible for my own happiness, not the salesman's. In fact, I couldn't care less whether or not the salesman is happy or likes me. And I don't have to buy anything I don't want.

In the beginning, most people find it helpful to keep track of all of this on paper. (I've included Cognitive Reframing Charts for your use at the end of this and other chapters.) With practice, it becomes easier and easier to dispute irrationalities in your head. Here's a brief excerpt from a session I recently had with a client in which I verbally guided him through the reframing process (the same process you can do on paper or in your head):

Dr. Z.: So you're worried about not being a good teacher.

Todd: That's right.

Dr. Z.: What is it specifically that worries you about not being a good teacher?

Todd: I feel that I have to be perfect, you know, give perfect lectures. If I make any mistakes, people will think I'm a lousy teacher.

Dr. Z.: So you can't stand the thought of being an imperfect teacher?

Todd: Yes.

Dr. Z.: You *demand* perfection from yourself, and you *require* that your teaching be eloquent, precise, accurate, and without flaw.

Todd: Yes.

Dr. Z.: And when you fail to do this, you feel like a *worthless, good-for-nothing bum.* And that's pretty *horrible* for you. Am I right?

Todd: You're right.

Dr. Z.: Just for the sake of argument, let's assume you really are a lousy teacher. A real loser. What's so horrible about that?

Todd: Well... I need to be perfect.

Dr. Z.: Who says you need to be perfect?

Todd: Uh... That's just the way I feel.

Dr. Z.: So *you're telling yourself* that you need to be perfect, and that it would be horrible if your teaching were anything less than perfect. Right?

Todd: Yeah, I guess. I still feel like people will think I'm a rotten teacher if I make mistakes.

Dr. Z.: Who says people will think you're a rotten teacher if you make mistakes?

Todd: I don't know, I just feel they will.

Dr. Z.: Again, *you're telling yourself* that other people will think or say this or that. Where's your proof?

Todd: I don't have any.

Dr. Z.: Additionally, why does it matter what they think?

Todd: I guess it really doesn't.

Dr. Z.: Bravo! If you'll recall, last time we talked about the concept of being a fallible human being? How might you apply this to your demands for self-perfection?

Todd: I suppose I could accept the fact that I'm human and going to make mistakes. A lot of mistakes. And that's okay. I could also quit rating myself according to what other people think or how well I teach.

Dr. Z.: You've got it.

Todd: It's hard, though.

Dr. Z.: You bet it is! But I'm sure you can do it, if you really want to change and you're willing to work at it.

So after filling out your chart or going through this type of dialogue once or twice (in your head or with a therapist), you're cured, right? Nice try, but no cigar! It'd be wonderful if life were that simple, but you and I know better. Cognitive restructuring takes time and a good deal of self-examination, but the rewards are definitely worth the degree of effort spent. I'll have more to say about making your reframes "stick" in Chapter 11, "Preparing for Battle."

COGNITIVE REFRAMING CHART

Situation:

Crazy-Maker:
Dispute:
Sensible Reply:

Situation:

Crazy-Maker:
Dispute:
Sensible Reply:

Situation:

Crazy-Maker:
Dispute:
Sensible Reply:

Situation:

Crazy-Maker:
Dispute:
Sensible Reply:

Situation:

Crazy-Maker:
Dispute:
Sensible Reply:

Chapter 4
Making What You Say and Do Count

Be obscure clearly.

— E. B. White

Now that we understand about the thinking part of psychological self-defense, let's learn about the saying and doing parts. In the next several pages, I'm going to introduce you to the principles of *effective communication,* the process whereby two or more people engage in meaningful, purposeful dialogue. Simply put, people who practice effective communication are on equal terms and say what they mean — neither party controls the conversation nor has hidden agendas. Knowledge and use of effective communication skills, coupled with rational thinking, is psychological self-defense at its best, giving you a powerful sense of control over your life and dealings with others.

Communication Patterns

Communication between people occurs in two ways: *verbal* (i.e., what we say) and *nonverbal* (i.e., what we do). Verbal messages come across through our words; nonverbal messages through our body posture, facial expressions, eye contact, hand gestures, touch, dress, and use of personal space. Both patterns occur simultaneously and involve a "sender" (source) conveying some type of information to a "receiver" (recipient), who in turn becomes a sender, etc., as dialogue continues. Sounds simple, right? Actually, there's much more to it than two people transmitting information back and forth like two computers. For example, the way something is said determines to a large extent the way the same is heard. That is, the *manner* in which the sender conveys information often affects the receiver's *interpretation* of the information.

Here's an example of how this works. A woman and her husband are sitting at breakfast, and he's reading the newspaper. His doing this every morning has bothered her for a long time, but she decides today is the day to say something. She then pulls the paper away from his face and screams, "Don't read the paper while we're eating!" He becomes angry and defensive, and the fireworks start. In this scenario, the woman's actions and raised voice imply, "I *demand* that you stop reading the paper, or else!" whereas all she really meant to say was, "I *prefer* that you not read the paper while we're eating."

In another version of this story, instead of screaming and grabbing the paper, the woman calmly says, "Dear, something's been bothering me about our breakfasts together. Are you willing to hear me out? Good! Well, sometimes I feel a little neglected when you read the paper at the table. Any chance we can talk about it, you know, maybe tonight?" Here, the woman's diplomacy and careful attention to non-verbal communication pays off by eliciting a completely different, this time cooperative, response from her husband.

In both cases, the verbal messages were essentially the same ("I don't want you to read the paper"); however, it was the combination of verbal and nonverbal messages in each case — the timing, actual words chosen, and the way the message was delivered — that were so strikingly different.

You can see from this example just how easy it is for communication to break down and become "faulty." Two of the most frequently encountered forms of *miscommunication* patterns couples engage in are *psychological games* and *mixed messages*.

Psychological games are the "roles" and "scripts" people assume in their relationships to keep from being themselves. By playing psychological games, people avoid dealing with personal and interpersonal issues and problems by not being straight with themselves or others. One example of a game is "Poor Me," in which an individual continually complains to get attention (James & Savary, 1976). Game-playing complicates interactions, and if left unchecked can even destroy a relationship.

People also frequently send out mixed messages, of which there are three types. In the first type, the sender says one thing verbally, but something entirely different with his or her body. An example of this is the person who says, "I'm listening to you" while looking off in another direction. The second type of mixed message involves conflicting verbal messages, an example being the person who says in one breath, "I like you," and in the next, "Get away from me." In the third type, the sender says two different things with his or her body. An example of this is the person who after being asked what she's feeling, says nothing, but smiles while clenching her fists.

One of the best ways to deal with psychological games and mixed messages (yours or anyone else's) is to accept the fact that they exist, and to work at catching yourself and others whenever these faulty patterns arise. Of course, you should be careful when you point out to others that they're playing games. If you're tactful and keep at it, though, you'll eventually reap the rewards of honest, open, and real communication.

Communication Skills and Self-Defense Responses (SDRs)

Central to keeping the lines of dialogue open between people are various verbal and nonverbal *communication skills,* which divide into two general groups: *sending skills* and *receiving skills.* When communication skills (both verbal and nonverbal) are used for purposes of psychological self-defense, I refer to them as *Self-Defense Responses* (SDRs).

Sending skills are communication skills that help the sender convey information about what he or she thinks, feels, or wants. Verbally, this is usually accomplished with I STATEMENTS, which reflect the sender's thoughts, feelings, and desires; PREFERENCE STATE-

MENTS, which reflect the sender's preferences; and BEHAVIOR STATEMENTS, which describe observable behaviors (Warren & Warren, 1985). As examples of these sending skills, consider the following dialogue:

> **Justin:** Sweetheart, I'm really pleased with our new car. (I STATEMENT)
> **Diane:** Me too, I'd like us to take a ride to see how it handles. (PREFERENCE STATEMENT)
> **Justin:** Yeah, sounds great! But I'd prefer we take it kind of slow to break the engine in. (PREFERENCE STATEMENT)
> **Diane:** Good idea. Let's go. (I STATEMENT)
> **Justin:** You know, I can tell you're happy. You're grinning from ear to ear. (BEHAVIOR STATEMENT)

Why are sending skills so important? Let's return to Justin and Diane, but this time consider what happens when they use ineffective sending skills:

> **Justin:** Sweetheart, I'm really pleased with our new car. (I STATEMENT)
> **Diane:** Yeah. (vague reply — impossible to determine the sender's motives)
> **Justin:** Is that all you have to say? You don't like our new car, do you? You never like anything I pick out. (accusing and blaming)
> **Diane:** I didn't say I don't like it. There you go again, putting words in my mouth. (more accusing and blaming)
> **Justin:** You're a real witch, Diane!
> **Diane:** Go jump in the lake, Justin!

The PREFERENCE STATEMENT is perhaps the most valuable sending skill a person can master. Instead of making *demands,* the individual states his or her *preferences.* Compare the following two statements and decide for yourself which is the more effective:

> **Justin:** I'd prefer we talk about the car some other time. (preferring)

versus

Justin: I'm sick of listening to you nag about the car. Why don't you just shut up! (demanding)

Two additionally important verbal communication skills are POSITIVE VERBAL TRACKING and POSITIVE VOCAL TRACKING. POSITIVE VERBAL TRACKING involves staying on the topic at hand, as there's little worse than feeling like you're not being heard because the other person keeps changing the subject. For example, two roommates having a disagreement about leaving the toilet seat up or down should do their best to stay on that topic until it is resolved. Moving too quickly to other topics only complicates matters, and might trigger a major argument.

The way in which something is said also affects how the other person will interpret a particular message. For example, loud, fast, high-pitched, blaring speech generally reflects anger; while soft, slow, low-pitched, steady speech generally reflects affection. POSITIVE VOCAL TRACKING, then, involves saying things in a such a way that the sender's true intent and interest come across to the receiver.

Receiving skills, the second major category of communication skills, help the receiver better understand the sender's message, as well as help the sender feel heard. In other words, receiving skills help you become a better listener. Only when each person believes he or she's being heard by the other can any meaningful dialogue take place. Valuable receiving skills include ENCOURAGING, PARA-PHRASING, DETAILING, and REALITY CHECKING.

ENCOURAGING includes using certain words and phrases to prompt the other person to continue talking. Brief utterances like "Uh-huh" and "Ummm," words like "Right" and "Yes," and phrases like "Tell me more" and "Keep going" help the other person feel he's being heard, as well as keeping the conversation moving. There are also a number of nonverbal encouragers, known as ENCOURAGING GESTURES (described below), that make verbal encouragers even more effective.

When PARAPHRASING, the receiver repeats back what she or he believes the sender has just said. PARAPHRASING does not involve word-for-word repetition, but instead picking up on and summarizing the most important points of the sender's message. Capturing both the content and feeling of what the sender is trying to communicate is central to good paraphrasing.

Here's an example of a listener using ENCOURAGING and PARAPHRASING to let her partner know she hears him and to keep their discussion moving:

> **Pavel:** Just stay out of my way. I had a really bad day today.
>
> **Mischa:** Tell me all about it. (ENCOURAGING)
>
> **Pavel:** First we had a pop quiz I wasn't prepared for in my economics class.
>
> **Mischa:** Uh-huh. (ENCOURAGING)
>
> **Pavel:** Then I got back my English paper — a big D- for all my trouble.
>
> **Mischa:** Ummm. (ENCOURAGING)
>
> **Pavel:** Then to top everything, the car wouldn't start, I had to call the auto club, and I was two hours late for work.
>
> **Mischa:** Two hours! Wow! (ENCOURAGING)
>
> **Pavel:** Yeah, I was so busy trying to get that stupid car taken care of, that I forgot to call my boss. They were freaking out by the time I got to the store. Mr. Henderson gave me a good chewing out — just what I needed today!
>
> **Mischa:** You poor guy! A pop test, a bad grade on your paper, the car not working, and late for work — all in the same day. No wonder you're upset. (PARAPHRASING)
>
> **Pavel:** You bet I'm upset... but thanks for listening. Guess I'll grab a bite to eat, take a hot shower, and go to bed. I'll just start over in the morning.
>
> **Mischa:** Sound's good. Let me know if there's anything I can do to help.

DETAILING involves asking the other person for more specific details concerning some point or issue he or she has raised. This technique is particularly useful when the other person is making generalizations about you or your behavior, and you want to help them identify specifics that you can both work with.

> **Mischa:** You're a blundering idiot!

Pavel: In what ways exactly am I a blundering idiot? (DETAILING)

REALITY CHECKING helps each person confirm the accuracy of his or her perceptions of the other's thoughts, feelings, needs, and wants. Here, each person periodically asks the other questions like, "Am I hearing you say that...?" or "I believe you said..., am I correct?" REALITY CHECKING is most effective when used immediately after PARAPHRASING. For instance:

> **Justin:** I'd prefer not to talk about your mother tonight. I'm exhausted and too mad about everything to make any sense. Anyway, when I'm like this... well, I don't want to say something I'll regret later. (I STATEMENT; PREFERENCE STATEMENT)
>
> **Diane:** Although I was hoping we'd be able to talk about Mom coming to visit, I hear you telling me you're really exhausted, angry, and afraid you might say something to me you'll regret. Am I hearing you straight? (PARAPHRASING; REALITY CHECKING)
>
> **Justin:** You're right on the money!

So far, we've primarily focused on verbal communication skills. But what about nonverbal skills? Do humans communicate in ways that don't involve words? Absolutely! In fact, psychological research clearly demonstrates that a great majority of people's communication occurs at a nonverbal level, i.e., with *body language*. When you think about it, we say so much with our bodies — how we really feel, our interest in whatever the partner is saying, our willingness to solve problems — all of which are reflected in the ways we look, sit, and move.

Body language as a communication skill involves three basic behaviors: POSITIVE EYE CONTACT, OPEN BODY POSTURE, and ENCOURAGING GESTURES. Generally speaking, Westerners consider it polite to maintain POSITIVE EYE CONTACT when conversing with others. Looking directly at the other person suggests interest in what's being said. Also, in Western cultures it is important to maintain an OPEN BODY POSTURE when communicating. This means sitting or standing in a relaxed manner, perhaps leaning for-

ward slightly, and uncrossing your arms and legs. Finally, ENCOUR-
AGING GESTURES are behaviors that encourage the other person to
continue talking. The most common of these for Westerners are head
nods and openhanded gestures, which can be particularly powerful
when used in conjunction with verbal ENCOURAGING (e.g., "Uh-
huh").

Chapter 5

Ready Replies

*Words are one of our chief means of adjusting to all
the situations of life. The better control we have over words,
the more successful our adjustment is likely to be.*

— Bergen Evans

"I get caught off-guard so easily. When I can't think, people
can talk me into anything."
"I'm a sucker when it comes to a slick sales pitch."
"I go blank when someone starts criticizing or poking fun at
me. I usually can't think of anything to say back, and I end up
feeling like a fool and getting down on myself."

These are only a few of the many remarks I hear from people who
have trouble "thinking on their feet" under the pressure of others'
demands, requests, commands, dictates, orders, requirements,
dictums, requests, petitions, and solicitations. And as I mentioned
earlier, this has been a special problem area in my life as well,
originally prompting me to develop the material for *Don't Let Them
Psych You Out!* as a way to protect myself. In this chapter, we
continue our discussion of making what you say and do count,
although now with a special emphasis on getting people to back off.

If you're one of those people who always gives in to others because you go blank under stress, then this chapter is for you. First off, I don't want to imply that everyone who asks you for a favor has devious motives and a hidden agenda. Many have good intentions, are honestly seeking your help, want what's best for all concerned, and don't mean to impose or make you uncomfortable. But then there's the other group — the ones who, no matter what they say, couldn't care less about you, your feelings, your finances, or your welfare. (If they did, they wouldn't be trying to pull nasty stuff on you in the first place, right?) They're deliberately trying to manipulate you. It's this second group that we're concerned with in this chapter.

One of the best ways to handle opponents during times of stress and going blank is to prepare yourself ahead of time with READY REPLIES (RRs). RRs are short, vague responses that you memorize and practice until you can spout them without having to think. Then, when you find yourself going blank, you still have something to say to divert your opponent until you can gather your thoughts and think your way out. The beauty of RRs lies in their simplicity — they're easy to learn and always there.

Be forewarned, however, about RRs and many of the other techniques I'll be presenting throughout this book. Because they are so powerful, there is a risk of your opponent becoming angry in response to your using them. So be careful about which technique you use with which opponent. Remember, the purpose of psychological self-defense isn't to elicit hostility, but to protect yourself. (I'll have more to say about assertion versus aggression in the next chapter.)

Where do I get my RRs? I believe the best RRs are the ones you make up yourself. They feel and sound more natural that way. I devise mine by thinking back on difficult situations I've suffered through and figuring out what verbal counters might have worked for me in those situations.

I'm particularly fond of RRs and other Self-Defense Responses that break the urgency of (URGENCY-BREAKING) or negate (NEGATING) my opponent's request; present an external reason why I can't do something (PASSING THE BUCK); or give me a chance to shift responsibility back to my opponent (RETURNING THE

MONKEY; I talk all about "Monkeys" in Chapter 7). Here are some examples of RRs from each of these categories:

Opponent: I must have an answer right now.
Dr. Z.: I'll have to think about it. (URGENCY-BREAKING)

and

Opponent: I must have an answer right now.
Dr. Z.: I'm not interested in your project. (NEGATING)

and

Opponent: I must have an answer right now.
Dr. Z.: I'm busy with a client and can't talk right now. (PASSING THE BUCK)

and

Opponent: I must have an answer right now.
Dr. Z.: Call me next week. (RETURNING THE MONKEY)
You can even combine RRs for greater effectiveness:

and

Opponent: I must have an answer right now.
Dr. Z.: Although I'm not very interested in your project, I'll think about it. I'm busy and can't talk right now, so call me next week. (URGENCY-BREAKING; NEGATING; PASSING THE BUCK; RETURNING THE MONKEY)

I'm also fond of RRs that are vague. The less clear, the better:

"Hmmm."
"I'm not sure."
"Really?"
"I don't know."
"Well, you know how it is."
"Sh** happens."
"That's life."
"Not now."
"Can't find good help these days."

Along these same lines, I find that trite, drained, overused, and meaningless platitudes, proverbs, clichés, euphemisms, and slogans make excellent RRs. These are some of my pets:

"Here today; gone tomorrow."
"Sauce for the goose."
"What goes up must come down."
"A stitch in time saves nine."
"Hard as a rock."
"Dead as a doornail."
"Easy come; easy go."
"Slowly but surely."
"It takes one to know one."

Now if you really want to confuse your opponent, try reversing the main parts of your proverbs and clichés. Then they become totally meaningless, but you'll sound like you're dropping "pearls of wisdom" (forgive the platitude!). Certainly your opponent will stop and ponder when he or she hears a REVERSE-ORDER READY REPLY like:

"Here tomorrow; gone today."
"What goes down must come up."
"A stitch in nine saves time."

Several years ago while in graduate school, I worked part-time in retail sales. A number of months into my job the boss hired the most obnoxious, irritating assistant manager imaginable. This woman was one of the angriest, nastiest people I'd ever met or had the displeasure of working under. And she hated men with a passion. Her strategy was to focus on each male employee and make his life so miserable that he'd eventually quit.

Well, she went through all the guys in the shop (who all quit within a couple of months), and then came my turn. This crazy woman was on my back from the minute I arrived at work until the minute I left. Nothing I did was right or enough. And neither the boss nor the district manager (both women) would do anything about the situation. Because I knew I was about to graduate and move on to bigger and better things, I chose to keep my cool and not explode while waiting things out. But to maintain some sense of sanity during my remaining weeks at the shop, I pulled the old proverb/cliché trick on her. Now keep in mind that I wasn't being aggressive or trying to upset the woman. But she hated it anyway! Although they didn't really solve my problem, my RRs did help me maintain at least some sense of control over a very miserable situation.

The best strategy when it comes to RRs, at least in the beginning, is to have a few general ones ready for use at all times. You want to keep things as simple and straightforward as possible — remember, you're trying to avoid mental confusion so that you can effectively handle opponent fire. If you spend too much time trying to decide which of 273 RRs you should use with the magazine solicitor at your door, you're needlessly complicating things.

In the chapters that follow, I'll be providing you with RRs for a variety of situations — RRs you can use directly or as models for devising your own. But before we move on, I'd like to leave you with four more examples of RRs in action:

Sara: On behalf of the alumni association here at Hoodwink University, it's my pleasure to inform you that you've been invited to join us as Chairperson of the Homecoming Dance. This is quite an honor, you know. Can we count on your being at our meeting this Wednesday night? Also, will you bring along refreshments for 30 or 40 people?
Tara: Doesn't sound like it's worth my time. Goodbye. (NEGATING)

and

Boss Bill: Your work is incompetent.
Employee Ed: Goose for the sauce. (REVERSE-ORDER READY REPLY)

and

Moe: I have this great wholesale grocery deal for you to look at. You can make a lot of money with this plan.
Joe: Put it in writing, and I'll run it past my friend who works for the IRS. (RETURNING THE MONKEY)

and

Betty: We need you to help us wrap Easter baskets next week. You're the only one we can count on.

Netty: My boss is keeping me really busy these days. (PASSING THE BUCK)

Chapter 6
Powerful
Assertiveness Techniques

The first and great commandment is, Don't let them scare you.

— Elmer Davis

Here are a few "soul-searching" questions for you:

- Do you ever get yourself into trouble by agreeing to do something before fully considering your options?
- Do people seem to gravitate to you for "favors" because they know you'll say YES?
- Do you ever feel guilty when you say NO?
- Do you ever just sit there and take your boss's fire because it's less scary than standing up to him or her?
- Do you ever feel like *they* know *they've* got you right where *they* want you?
- Do you believe that people take advantage of you because you're good-natured?
- Do people push you around because they know they can get away with it?
- Do you hate taking a defective product back to the store because you're afraid the salesperson will get mad?

• Do you dread causing a scene in public?

If after taking an honest look at your life, you answered YES to one or more of these questions, you may have fallen into the trap of being *nonassertive*. Nonassertiveness, the opposite of assertiveness or assertion, involves failure to acknowledge one's personal rights and responsibilities. Nonassertive people rarely stand up for themselves when faced with others' demands, criticisms, and manipulations. They tend to be reserved and apologetic, as well as unrealistically concerned about offending others. They also downplay their own needs, wants, and goals. Assertive people, on the other hand, believe in their right to express themselves in whatever manner they choose, so they're always quick to voice their opinions, thoughts, and preferences. They stand up to others, take up for themselves, confront others' manipulations, and make sure their needs are met (though not at anyone else's expense). Assertive people also respect the rights of other people to do the same, and they appreciate the fact that everyone is entitled to differing opinions.

Nonassertiveness is central to many people's unhappiness and emotional turmoil. Why? Because people *choose* if and when they will be assertive or not. No one *forces* anyone to be one way or the other. Realistically, you basically have four options when faced with a potential or real threat: 1) fight your opponent, 2) back down, 3) escape from the conflict altogether, or 4) be assertive. Most people make use of the first three options, especially "backing down." The purpose of *Don't Let Them Psych You Out!*, then, is to help you see the value of exercising the fourth option — "being assertive" — which is what psychological self-defense is all about.

Before I introduce specific assertiveness techniques, let's consider why most people prefer to avoid standing up to others. Below are five typical Crazy-Makers (CMs) people have about being assertive:

1. People won't like me if I disagree with or stand up to them.
2. It's impolite to challenge others.
3. If I talk back to my boss, I'll get fired.
4. What would other people think if I made a scene in public?
5. If I let go, I'm afraid I'll lose control, and maybe even hurt the other person.

Below are sample Disputes and Sensible Replies (SRs) for these CMs:

Dispute: Who cares if people don't like me when I disagree with them?
SR: Not me! I like myself, and that's what really matters.

and

Dispute: Where's the rule that says it's impolite to challenge others?
SR: As an assertive person, I can say whatever I feel is necessary, especially if someone is taking advantage of me.

and

Dispute: What's the probability that I'll be fired if I talk back to my boss?
SR: There's always a possibility I'll be fired, but the probability is small or nil. And even if I were fired, it'd be inconvenient, not awful. Anyway, who wants to work for a boss who doesn't respect his employees' integrity?

and

Dispute: What difference does it make what other people think?
SR: If I want to make a scene in public, that's my business. I'm not any less of a person if people don't approve of me or my actions.

and

Dispute: What's the chance I'll lose control and hurt the other person?
SR: There's always a possibility, but the probability is small or nil. Using psychological self-defense gives me control over myself and my interactions with others, so I never need to resort to violence or aggression unless I choose to.

This last example brings to mind a common falsehood — that being *assertive* is the same as being *aggressive*. Aggressiveness involves intentional attempts to belittle, insult, hurt, malign, or destroy someone or something. People generally express aggressiveness through sarcasm, put-downs, negative labels, and hostile words and actions. None of this has anything to do with assertiveness. Here's an example of the differences between the two:

> **Jim:** Will you do me a favor and videotape my wedding next week?
> **Dean:** Hell no! (being aggressive)

> *versus*

> **Dean:** No offense, but I'd rather not. Anyway, I know there are professional photographers listed in the phone book who hire out to tape special events. Please give my best to your bride-to-be. (being assertive)

It's apparent from this example that you need not be offensive or rude to be assertive. Actually, I believe it's more efficient and effective to be *politely* assertive, although whether or not you choose to do this depends on your particular situation, personal style, and mood at the time. If you choose to be assertive with someone, but you're also feeling angry or annoyed, keep in mind the old saying, "It's easier to attract ants with honey than with vinegar."

There may be times, though, when some degree of aggression is called for. My brother Steve relayed a story to me about an experience he had some years ago with a manager at a fast food restaurant where he worked. This 16-year-old manager continually criticized, insulted, and embarrassed my brother in front of the customers. Steve, being a fairly patient individual, kept letting it slide. Then he tried assertively talking things out, but nothing seemed to work. One day, Steve had had it, and decided a little aggression was in order. He grabbed the manager by the shirt, pushed him against the wall, and told him that if he ever embarrassed him in front of the customers again, he'd break his neck. To say the least, this ended the problem. And interestingly enough, the two eventually became the best of friends. So yes, a little aggression can go a long way in some cases, although I (like my brother) believe it's usually best to exercise all other options first.

I'd like to mention one final point before moving on to specific assertiveness techniques. Be careful about giving reasons for why you do or don't want to do something. First, it's nobody's business what your reasons are. You don't have to explain anything to anybody. Second, giving reasons and explaining often come across to others as *excuses*. Many opponents will do their best to invalidate your excuses as a way of talking you into doing what they want. Consider the following:

> **Sam:** So Dave, can I borrow your new car tonight?
> **Dave:** Well, the engine's not broken in, and I might need it tonight, and...
> **Sam:** You worry wart! I'll take it easy, you know, drive it under 40 mph all evening — I promise. And my sister can give you a lift in my jalopy tonight if you need a ride somewhere. What do you say?
> **Dave:** Okay I guess. But...
> **Sam:** Thanks, guy!

versus

> **Sam:** Dave, can I borrow your new car tonight?
> **Dave:** To tell you the truth, I never lend out my car.
> **Sam:** Why not?
> **Dave:** I just never lend out my car.
> **Sam:** But why?
> **Dave:** I just never lend out my car.
> **Sam:** Don't you trust me?
> **Dave:** Sure I trust you. I just never lend out my car.
> **Sam:** Well... okay. Thanks anyway.

In the first example, Sam puts nonassertive Dave on the defensive, prompting Dave to shuffle around for some plausible excuses not to lend Sam his new car. (Spur-of-the moment excuses are usually pretty weak.) In the second example, however, assertive Dave puts Sam on the defensive, prompting Sam to give up asking for the car. Amazing what a big difference a small shift in attitude and words can make!

The Sam and Dave example above demonstrates one of my favorite assertion techniques — the TAPE LOOP. This simple, yet powerful, technique involves repeating the same word or sentence over and over again, irrespective of your opponent's remarks. And there's no beating the TAPE LOOP if you're persistent; your opponent backs himself into a corner every time! The TAPE LOOP works something like this:

Dr. Z.: I'm returning this briefcase. I want my money back.

Salesperson: What's wrong with it?

Dr. Z.: It's scratched on the outside.

Salesperson: What? That little scratch? Man, my briefcase has lots of scratches bigger than this one.

Dr. Z.: Nevertheless, I'm returning this briefcase. I want my money back. (TAPE LOOP)

Salesperson: Wouldn't you rather keep it? It's a nice briefcase.

Dr. Z.: No, I want my money back. (TAPE LOOP)

Salesperson: Unfortunately, the assistant manager, manager, vice president, and CEO will all need to approve the return. I won't even be able to get to it for hours. Why don't you just come back next week, okay?

Dr. Z.: I want my money back, and I want you deal with my refund now. (TAPE LOOP)

Salesperson: I'm really busy now. I'm sorry, there are other people waiting behind you. Please move aside. You're holding up the line.

Dr. Z.: (still standing there) I want my money back, and I want you to deal with my refund now. (TAPE LOOP)

Salesperson: The other customers are getting angry.

Dr. Z.: I don't care about the other customers. I want my money back, and I want you to deal with my refund now. (TAPE LOOP)

Salesperson: Okay, enough already.

This situation occurred in Houston many years ago. The salesman tried every line in the book to get me to leave, hoping I'd just forget the whole thing and not bother coming back. Instead, I stood my ground, and received the prompt refund I'd requested.

Perhaps the most fundamental of all assertiveness tactics is saying NO. That's right, NO! Why is saying NO so basic? Because it's one of the first words we ever hear as children. We learn from hearing NO that we can't always have our way, that life doesn't always give us everything we want. For these reasons, the word NO is emotionally loaded, carrying a lot of negative associations for most people. That's why so many nonassertive folks hate to say NO. They're afraid of rejection, disappointing others, triggering an uncomfortable scene or conflict, etc. — their fears and insecurities tracing back to negative experiences during childhood or adolescence.

Fortunately, all's not lost, my friend. Regardless of your early life experiences, you can learn to say NO, and learn to say it with gusto and resolve!

I find it helpful to distinguish between two types of NOs: NICE NOs and BLUNT NOs. The former NOs are cordial and gentle, the latter direct and to-the-point, as the following demonstrate:

Carla: Beth, can I borrow $20?
Beth: I'd rather not, Carla. (NICE NO)

versus

Carla: Beth, can I borrow $20?
Beth: No! No!! No!!! (BLUNT NO)

I personally prefer to use NICE NOs whenever possible (my being ever the diplomat!). Why? Because I find that people generally respond more favorably to less brutal NOs; but again, this is my personal style. You may find using BLUNT NOs to be more to your liking and personality. Be sure to consider the potential BLUNT NOs have to elicit hostility on the part of your opponent.

> **Rob:** Bob, the company needs you to donate money each month from your check to so-and-so's charity. It's only a couple of bucks, and you won't even miss it. What do you say?
> **Bob:** No thanks. (NICE NO)
> **Rob:** Oh come on, Bob. It's for a good cause.

Bob: No thanks. (NICE NO; TAPE LOOP)
Rob: But everyone else is giving. You wouldn't want people
to think you're tight or stingy, would you?
Bob: No thanks. (NICE NO; TAPE LOOP)

Rob will never get anywhere with this approach as long as Bob
keeps using his NICE NOs and the TAPE LOOP. But what if Bob
gets sick and tired of being hounded and bombarded with questions?
Bob might try using one or two BLUNT NOs, with appropriate
changes in his vocal tone:

Rob: Quit resisting, Bob. You know you'll eventually give in
to me. You always do. Come on, give a donation.
Bob: (raising his voice slightly) How many times do I have to
tell you something? I said NO! (BLUNT NO; POSITIVE
VOCAL TRACKING)
Rob: What?
Bob: (raising his voice considerably): I said NO, NO, NO!!!
Got it? NO!!! (BLUNT NO; POSITIVE VOCAL TRACK-
ING)

Unless Rob is an imbecile (and some opponents are), he'll back
off at this point, especially as other people in the office begin to take
notice. A good, strong NO can work wonders in even the most
exploitative and pressured of situations.

Related to NICE NOs and BLUNT NOs is LIMIT-SETTING.
With this technique, you indirectly say NO by setting your boundaries
and refusing to budge. LIMIT-SETTING replies often go something
like this:

"I don't feel comfortable doing this."
"I won't agree to that."
"That's not my way of doing things."
"I won't cross that line."
"I'll do this, but not that."

Here's an example of the power of LIMIT-SETTING and the
TAPE LOOP used in combination:

Jan: I want you to call me every night of the week.

Dean: No thanks. I don't feel comfortable doing that. I'll call you once a week, but not every night. (NICE NO; LIMIT-SETTING)

Jan: But why? Don't you love me?

Dean: I do love you. But I still don't feel comfortable with the idea of calling you every night. I'll call you once a week. (LIMIT-SETTING; TAPE LOOP)

Jan: Then what about calling me every other night?

Dean: Like I said, I'll call you once a week. (LIMIT-SETTING; TAPE LOOP)

Jan can pester Dean to change his mind until the cows come home, but it won't do her any good as long as he uses LIMIT-SETTING and the TAPE LOOP.

One warning, however, when it comes to NOs and LIMIT-SETTING. Once you've said NO, *never, never reconsider or change your answer to YES!,* no matter how hard your opponent works you over. If you give in, even once, your opponent will never take you at your word again. He knows if he keeps after you, you'll eventually cave in. So only use NOs or LIMIT-SETTING when you really mean it. Otherwise use a vague READY REPLY or other technique until you decide what you really want.

With the TAPE LOOP, NICE NOs, BLUNT NOs, and LIMIT-SETTING in hand (and with even more exciting assertiveness techniques to follow in upcoming chapters), maybe you're ready for something a little different? How about a chapter on monkeys?

Chapter 7

Where's the Monkey?

I confess freely to you, I could never look long
upon a monkey without very mortifying reflections.
— **William Congreve**

As part of a discussion group early in my clinical internship, one of our staff psychologists asked all of us interns what kind of animal we'd like to be if we could change. Most of the interns chose solemn, stately animals — eagles, peacocks, cats, and the like. But what animal did yours truly pick? You guessed it — a *monkey!* The psychologist chuckled (as did the other interns), and probed further:

Dr. W.: A monkey? Why a monkey?
Me: I like the sound they make when they laugh and howl.
Dr. W.: What would you do as a monkey?
Me: I'd really like to swing by my tail on a chandelier during a stuffy, formal dinner or reception.
Dr. W.: (no answer)

Needless to say, from that moment on I was branded a "friendly" rebel at the clinic, a reputation I hold there even today.

So what's my reason for bringing up this seemingly pointless story? I love monkeys. I always have. They're intelligent, lively, and playful. But as pets they can be a pain in the neck. And so can the "monkeys" you'll run across, not in zoos, but in your everyday dealings. Have I lost you yet? Let me explain.

"There's a monkey on your back" is a popular phrase in the field of management. A "monkey" in management lingo refers to an "agreed upon responsibility." Whoever has the monkey on his or her back has agreed to be responsible for doing something. For example, if I tell you I'll phone you next week, I've put a monkey on my back. If I ask you to phone me next week, and you agree, you've put a monkey on your back (with my help, of course).

Have you surmised how monkeys fit into a psychological self-defense program? One of the cleverest moves an opponent can make is to convince you to put his monkey on your back. It's a slick way of shifting responsibility from him to you. The more monkeys you have, the less your opponent has, which is exactly what he wants. Why? Because when you take his monkeys, he has less responsibility and more free time — courtesy of your good intentions!

Please don't misunderstand. Not everyone who tries to put a monkey on your back has nefarious motives. Not everyone is trying to move work from their desk to yours. Many nice people unintentionally offer you monkeys. But just because there isn't sinister intent doesn't mean you *have* to accept the monkeys people give you. There's no law that says you *must* take on anyone else's projects and responsibilities. You probably have enough monkeys of your own to take care of without taking on any more.

And now for some particulars. There are three parts to this monkey business (pun intended!). Here's how it usually works (from one of my many real-life monkey examples):

1. Your opponent first tries to give you a monkey.

> **Student:** Dr. Z, will you mail me a copy of your latest article when you get back to the university next month?
> **Dr. Z.:** Well, I'll probably forget to send it to you by the time I get back to Oregon.

Student: I know you won't forget. It's very important to me. Here's my address.

In this case, the student wants to give Dr. Z. her monkey. But Dr. Z. doesn't want to hold onto an address, or try to remember to mail an article a month later. It's now up to Dr. Z. to decide to accept or refuse the monkey.

2. You either accept or refuse the monkey.

Student: Dr. Z, will you mail me a copy of your latest article when you get back to the university next month?
Dr. Z.: Sure. (ACCEPTING THE MONKEY)

versus

Dr. Z.: No, I'm sure I'll forget. Tell you what. I'll be happy to mail you the article if you'll write or call me at the university after I've returned to my office. That way I'll be able to tend to it right then and there. (REFUSING THE MONKEY)

If the person keeps after you, you can use some of your other assertiveness skills to refuse the monkey.

Student: Oh please, Dr. Z. Please send me your article. It's so important. You couldn't possibly forget.
Dr. Z.: Again, I have to say No. I'm sure I'll forget. You seem to be very intent on convincing me to remember to send you the article. If it's that important to you, why do you object to writing or calling me for it later? (NICE NO; TAPE LOOP; PROCESS COMMENT, described in the next chapter)

3. You return the monkey that you no longer want.

Student: Thanks for agreeing to send me your article.
Dr. Z.: You know, the more I think about it, the more uncomfortable I feel about trying to remember to send you my article. I'd rather not have to think about it over my vacation. Instead, I'll be happy to send it to you if you'll call or write me at my office when I get back. (RETURNING THE MONKEY)

Let's take another monkey example, this one excerpted from one of my therapy sessions:

Client: Your therapy is useless! It hasn't helped me one bit!!!

Dr. Z.: Really? (READY REPLY)

Client: Yeah, I don't see any reason to spend $3 per hour (this was a low-income, reduced-fee client) to see a psychologist, especially you.

Dr. Z.: Hmmm. (RR)

Client: Well, what are you going to do to make me feel better?

Dr. Z.: The question is, what are *you* going to do to make *yourself* feel better? (REFUSING THE MONKEY)

Client: But you're the doctor! You're supposed to fix my life.

Dr. Z.: Really? (RR)

Client: I pay good money to come in here and have you fix my life, which you haven't done. Do something for a change, instead of just telling me to change how I think.

Dr. Z.: You know I can't fix your life. Only you can do that.

Client: Then why am I coming here?

Dr. Z.: Because the court requires you to see me. Hopefully, though, you're also here to learn how to fix your own life rather than expecting someone else to.

Client: But you're the doctor. You're supposed to make me feel better.

Dr. Z.: Yes, I'm the doctor. But it's not my place to make you feel better. Even if I could, I wouldn't. That's your job. I can only act as your coach. (REFUSING THE MONKEY)

Client: I'm not ever coming back here, and it's your fault.

Dr. Z.: It's up to you and your parole officer whether or not you'll have to come back to the clinic. As for blaming me for your miseries, I don't accept credit for my clients' successes or blame for their failures. (REFUSING THE MONKEY)

I'm sure you get the idea from the above dialogue that this was an especially difficult court-mandated client. Nonetheless, it's an excellent example of one person trying to give monkeys to another, who in turn refuses them.

In sum, the three most important things to remember about monkeys are 1) that they exist, 2) that people might try to put them on your back, and 3) that your opponent's monkeys belong on your opponent's back, not on yours. Keeping mindful of the potential for an opponent to give away monkeys will help you avoid running a primate house in your spare time.

Chapter 8
Unconventional
Strategies

Custom does often reason overrule
and only serves for reason to the fool.
— **John Wilmot, Earl of Rochester**

As an assertive but fallible individual, you have the following rights and responsibilities:

- You have the right to think, feel, say, and do whatever you choose, (within the limits of the law, of course) regardless of what others think, feel, say, and do.
- You have the responsibility to live with the consequences of your choices and actions.
- You have the right to set your own limits.
- You have the responsibility to respect the limits others set for themselves.
- You have the right to say NO to others' requests and demands.
- You have the responsibility to allow others to say NO to you.
- You have the right to form and voice your own opinions.
- You have the responsibility to respect others' opinions, even if they differ from your own.

- You have the right to find your own answers and solutions to problems.
- You have the responsibility to permit others to find their own answers and solutions.
- You have the right to fulfill your own needs, and not feel guilty about it.
- You have the responsibility to let others fulfill their own needs.
- You have the right to not know everything.
- You have the responsibility to respect others when they don't know everything.
- You have the right to make mistakes and learn from them.
- You have the responsibility to allow others to make their own mistakes.
- And last but not least, you have the right to be imperfect when it comes to the above rights and responsibilities.

In order to realize these assertion rights and responsibilities, there may be times when you choose to break away from "custom" and use one or more *unconventional* psychological self-defense strategies. By this I mean strategies that transcend the usual rules of conversational etiquette and politeness. In other words, instead of *effective communication,* you deliberately practice what at first would seem to be *ineffective communication.* That doesn't mean your encounters will be ineffective. When used properly, unconventional strategies can be some of your most powerful self-defense weapons. On the downside, however, because they can be so powerful, unconventional strategies also carry the greatest potential to anger your opponents. Be forewarned!

One unconventional, though not always appreciated, Self-Defense Response is INTERRUPTING (also termed CHANGING THE SUBJECT and NEGATIVE VERBAL TRACKING). Here, you purposely interrupt and change the subject while someone else is talking. INTERRUPTING is especially effective against long-winded or annoying monologues and one-way conversations. Your opponent's typical response to INTERRUPTING will be to go along, especially if the INTERRUPTING takes the form of a request or question. Here's an example:

Moe: My latest book on microcomputer chips is so fascinating. Let me tell you all about it. In the first chapter, I...

Joe: Excuse me, Moe, will you please get me a soda? My blood sugar is dropping. (INTERRUPTING)

Moe: Sure thing.

and

Moe: Here's your soda. I hope you feel better. Now back to my book. In the first chapter, I...

Joe: Excuse me again, Moe. I didn't realize the time. I've got to get back to work now. How about you? Have you finished that report yet? (INTERRUPTING)

Moe: No, I haven't. I guess I better get back to work, too.

Joe: Yeah. Talk to you later.

INTERRUPTING is an excellent "on-the-spot" technique. And in many cases, the opponent moves on to something else. If, however, he or she keeps after you, you might try NEGATING. For example:

Moe: Finally, we're alone and both have time for me tell you about my book. In the first chapter, I...

Joe: No offense, Moe, but I'm not really interested in hearing about your book right now. (NEGATING)

Assertive people also use NEGATIVE VOCAL TRACKING to make a point, diffuse uncomfortable situations, and regain control in a conflict. Here, you use an unexpected vocal tone to make your point. For example, if you raise your voice at me, you're probably expecting me to do the same in return. What if I don't? What would you do if after yelling at me, I gave you a quiet, peaceful reply? Or what would you do if after quietly asking me for a favor, I responded with an excessively loud NO!? I think you see my point. There's no rule that says you have to respond the way the other person wants or expects you to.

Another unconventional Self-Defense Response is the PROCESS COMMENT. Psychologists and other mental health specialists frequently distinguish between CONTENT and PROCESS remarks. A CONTENT COMMENT is a response to what is *apparently* being said (i.e., the particular words used to express an idea).

Frick: You're rude, crude, and I don't like you!
Frack: What do you mean *I'm* rude and crude? *You're* no prize yourself, bud. I don't like *you* either. (CONTENT COMMENT)

and

Salesman: You seem like a very sophisticated shopper who knows how to find a bargain.
Customer: Why thank you! I guess I'm pretty good at finding a bargain. (CONTENT COMMENT)

On the other hand, a PROCESS COMMENT is a response to what is *really* being said (i.e., the underlying message behind the actual words chosen). It involves interpreting the content of the sender's statements in light of what you believe is his or her true intent. You essentially read "between the lines" when making a PROCESS COMMENT.

Frick: You're rude, crude, and I don't like you!
Frack: You must still be upset about losing all that money in the poker game last week. (PROCESS COMMENT)

and

Salesman: You seem like a very sophisticated shopper who knows how to find a bargain.
Customer: You seem like a very insincere salesman who wants to flatter me into buying something I don't need. (PROCESS COMMENT)

As you might imagine, PROCESS COMMENTS are excellent for cutting through garbage and getting to the sender's true message. Because the PROCESS COMMENT tends to throw an opponent "off center" (at least temporarily), it quickly puts an end to unwelcome criticism, shifty sales ploys, and other underhanded manipulations.

Another jewel is the REFLECTING QUESTION, or the "What-Is-It-About...?" counter. The REFLECTING QUESTION capitalizes on the premise that good people always respond whenever spoken to. With this one, you repeat back everything your opponent says in the form of a question, which he or she feels compelled to answer.

Rick: I can't stand domestic cars. Why do you drive a domestic car?

Nick: What is it about domestic cars that you don't like? (REFLECTING QUESTION)

Rick: They're too expensive for what you get.

Nick: What is it about their being too expensive that you don't like? (REFLECTING QUESTION)

Rick: Well, they don't work right.

Nick: What is it about their not working right that you don't like? (REFLECTING QUESTION)

Rick: They're always in the shop.

Nick: What is it about their always being in the shop that you don't like? (REFLECTING QUESTION)

Rick: It's too expensive to keep them going.

Nick: What is it about their being too expensive that you don't like? (REFLECTING QUESTION)

Rick: Forget I brought it up. Man, you've got some problems!

Nick: What is about my having problems that you don't like? (REFLECTING QUESTION)

And so the conversation goes (forever if need be). Your opponent will probably keep trying to answer for a while, but will soon give up when it becomes apparent he isn't getting anywhere. The REFLECTING QUESTION is exceptionally good for dealing with unfriendly criticism, which is described more fully in Chapter 15.

Four final techniques I'd like to mention are AGREEING, DISAGREEING, FLATTERING, and the SMART ALECK. I don't tend to use any of these (they're far too insincere for my tastes), but they may fit your needs.

AGREEING involves exactly what it says — *agreeing with everything* your opponent says or asks, even if you don't believe for a minute what you agree to or intend to follow through with your opponent's demands. Here's an example of AGREEING:

Daisy: You're looking tacky today, aren't you?

Maisy: You're right, I'm looking tacky today. (AGREEING)

Daisy: Your shoes don't even match your dress.

Maisy: You're right, my shoes don't match my dress. (AGREEING)

Daisy: Why don't you go and buy another outfit, or can't you afford to buy *new* clothes?

Maisy: I was planning to buy a new outfit, but you're right, I can only afford to buy *used* clothes. (AGREEING)

Daisy: What, your good-for-nothing husband doesn't make enough money?

Maisy: Yeah, my good-for-nothing husband doesn't make enough money. (AGREEING)

Daisy: I really feel sorry for you.

Maisy: I really feel sorry for me, too. (AGREEING)

Daisy: Oh, by the way, will you pick me up tomorrow night to go to the PTA meeting? I'd hate to waste my gas.

Maisy: I'd be more than happy to pick you up tomorrow night. I'd also hate for you to waste your gas. (AGREEING)

In this example, Maisy doesn't care if what she says to Daisy is sincere or not. And of course, neither does she bother to pick up Daisy the next evening, even though she said she would. Because Daisy is attempting to belittle and insult Maisy, Maisy does what she feels is necessary to deal with Daisy's cutting remarks and demands. Do you think Daisy might learn a lesson from this episode, particularly if Maisy confronts Daisy after she's had a little time to think about the situation, like after waiting for the ride that never comes?

Along similar lines, DISAGREEING involves *disagreeing with everything* your opponent says or asks. For instance:

Ned: The political system in this country is about to collapse.

Jed: I disagree. (DISAGREEING)

Ned: What do you mean you disagree? All politicians are crooks, and the people are on the verge of revolution.

Jed: I don't believe that. (DISAGREEING)

Ned: What are you, crazy? Can't you see that the people are fed up with inflation, unemployment, and our rundown health care system?

Jed: I don't believe that either. (DISAGREEING)

Ned: You really are nuts.

Jed: Not really. (DISAGREEING)
Ned: Okay, smart guy, just for the sake of argument, let's say you're right, that everything is okay.
Jed: I don't believe that either. (DISAGREEING)
Ned: What? Man, you don't make any sense!
Jed: I disagree. (DISAGREEING)
Ned: Just forget I said anything.

Your opponent gets nowhere fast when you intentionally agree or disagree with everything he says. If he's got any sense at all, he'll leave you alone.

When FLATTERING, you pay your opponent all kinds of compliments, which you may or may not mean or believe. Your purpose is to massage your opponent's ego to get him or her off your back. Here's an example of FLATTERING:

Jill: You botched up the party napkins. Can't you do anything right?
Dill: You know, that's a very beautiful outfit you have on. Where did you buy it? (FLATTERING)
Jill: Oh, this thing? Actually, I bought it at the most expensive store in town.
Dill: Well, you look just great. Am I jealous! (FLATTERING)
Jill: Why thank you! You know, on second thought, I think the party napkins will do just fine. How about if I treat you to lunch?

Another unconventional Self-Defense Response is the SMART ALECK. With this one, you respond to whatever your opponent says with conceited and pretentiously clever remarks. For instance:

Bob: I'm so wonderful. Everything I do is marvelous. I'm super intelligent, suave, and...
Carol: And modest, too. (SMART ALECK)
Bob: As I was saying, I'm brilliant, handsome, and always the life of the party.
Carol: What, am I supposed to feel sorry for you, or something? (SMART ALECK)
Bob: At least I have personality.

Carol: Oh, is that what you call it? (SMART ALECK)

Many of the techniques I've described in this and previous chapters take advantage of an irrational assumption prevalent among Westerners: *that every question must be answered, and that you're impolite and rude if you don't.* If I direct a malicious comment your way, you're *supposed* to go on the defensive and answer. In effect, I'm manipulating you into either taking my guff or defending yourself. Either way, I'm controlling you and your reactions. "But what am I supposed to do, ignore the other person? I can't do that," you may be asking. Sure you can (as we'll see in the next chapter). Or respond, if that's what you want to do. But do it because you *choose* to, not because you think you *have* to.

Chapter 9

Silence is Golden!

They talk most who have the least to say.
— **Matthew Prior**

In this chapter, I'm going to let you in on one of the most powerful of all psychological Self-Defense Responses — SILENCE! That's right. Dead quiet. Verbal stillness. A held tongue. Peace, hush, and dumbness. However you describe it, SILENCE boils down to one thing — *keeping your mouth shut,* even when you feel you *should* say something merely because you think your opponent expects it!

Psychologists refer to deliberate, intentional SILENCE as *selective inattention,* a fancy term for ignoring clients' inappropriate statements and behaviors. For example, a therapist might use selective inattention to discourage a depressed client from bringing up the same negative topics over and over again. By not paying attention to undesirable words and actions, the therapist avoids reinforcing them, and the client is then less likely to continue exhibiting them. Sound reasonable? Trust me, it's a powerful therapeutic technique.

Having encountered many opponents in my day, it finally occurred to me, "If selective inattention works so well with my clients, why not use it with my opponents? I mean, we all fall into the trap of acting and reacting according to what we believe are society's expectations. Why not also throw out those irrational ideas about *having* to answer questions or respond to nonsensical remarks?" *Bingo!* I had found my answer for dealing with those particularly problematic opponents — intentional SILENCE!

At this point, you're probably thinking, "You mean if someone asks me a question I don't like or demands that I do something I don't want to, I can just stand or sit there and say nothing?" Exactly!!! *Because —*

- You don't *have* to answer to anyone, including your opponent!
- You don't *need* to explain yourself to anyone, including your opponent!
- You don't *have* to acknowledge anyone, *especially* your opponent!!!

"But won't people think I'm rude if I remain silent?" *Who cares?*
"But isn't it impolite to ignore people?" *Where's the rule?*
"But won't people hate me if I refuse to answer them?" *So what if they do?*

Intentional SILENCE is a difficult concept for most people in our culture. It goes against everything that we're taught as children and teenagers. Old patterns are hard to break, *but they can be broken* as long as you're motivated and willing to work at it. (I've included some exercises at the end of this chapter to help you become more at ease using intentional SILENCE.)

"Isn't this too good to be true?" you wonder. "Isn't this too simple to work?" you ask. My response to you, friend, is this: no one said psychological self-defense has to be complicated to be effective. In all truth, the simpler your strategies, the better. However, don't let the mere simplicity of SILENCE fool you. SILENCE may be an uncomplicated technique, but it's not necessarily an easy one, especially in the beginning. In fact, the skillful use of SILENCE is probably the hardest technique in this book to master.

That said, how does SILENCE work as a self-defense strategy? Because one example is worth a thousand words, consider the following dialogue:

Neighbor A: Hey, you. Keep your dog off my lawn!
Neighbor B: (doesn't look at or respond to Neighbor A) (SILENCE)
Neighbor A: Didn't you hear me, you moron? I said keep your dog off my lawn!
Neighbor B: (continues to ignore Neighbor A, and then goes into the house) (SILENCE)
Neighbor A: (looking very confused) Didn't you... Uh? Oh well.

Here's another example:

Bar Patron 1: You know something, stranger, you're ugly and you drink like a wimp.
Bar Patron 2: (doesn't look at or respond to the other guy) (SILENCE)
Bar Patron 1: We don't like strangers in here. I said you're ugly and a wimp.
Bar Patron 2: (still ignoring the other guy) (SILENCE)
Bar Patron 1: Didn't you hear me? I called you ugly and a wimp!
Bar Patron 2: (still silent) (SILENCE)
Bar Patron 1: Man, are you deaf?
Bar Patron 2: (silently finishes his drink and walks out of the bar) (SILENCE)
Bar Patron 1: (looking dumbfounded, says to the bartender) Ah, that one wasn't even worth beating up.

Notice how in these two examples, deliberate SILENCE helps the "attacked" individuals maintain a sense of self-control in light of potential conflicts and protect themselves psychologically (and maybe physically, too, if a conflict were to escalate to the point of throwing punches). The opponents are at a loss as to how to respond, because they (like the rest of us) have been conditioned to expect others to answer or get defensive when attacked. When they don't, the opponents feel threatened and insecure. Their manipulating, invalidating manner of interacting with others has failed them, and they may question the very core of their life assumptions. And all because someone didn't bother acknowledging them or their remarks!

SILENCE is great against all kinds of verbal attacks, but especially criticisms, invalidations, and hostile remarks. And besides being profoundly effective, SILENCE is available anytime, anywhere. In upcoming chapters, we'll see how to use SILENCE to counter opponents in a variety of situations.

Two variations on the SILENCE routine are the STARE and the ICE-COLD GLARE. With both of these, you don't verbally say anything to your opponent; you instead *stare* or *glare* at him. When you use the STARE, you have a blank, emotionless expression on your face (what psychologists call a *flat effect*). When you use the ICE-COLD GLARE, you *sneer* a little, which in no uncertain terms lets the other person know that you're annoyed. Regardless of the variation used, your opponent will get the message that you couldn't care less about what he thinks, says, feels, or does. Here's the ICE-COLD GLARE in action:

> **Student:** You're not fair! You can't even teach!
> **Teacher:** (remains silent; doesn't look up at the student while continuing to work in her office) (SILENCE)
> **Student:** I said you're a lousy teacher!
> **Teacher:** (still silent and working) (SILENCE)
> **Student:** Did you hear me? You're lousy!
> **Teacher:** (still silent, but now looking up and sneering at the student) (ICE-COLD GLARE)
> **Student:** Never mind. I'll come back some other time.

I promise you, this one works nearly every time. There's nothing more intimidating for most folks than to have their verbal blurts meet a silent, sneering glare. Why? Because silence, sneers, and glares translate into *disapproval,* which if it happens to us is supposed to be *terrible.* That's what we're taught from day one as children. Further, when on the receiving end of SILENCE, people feel uncomfortable and out of control of their situation. So they desperately try to gain control by arguing, shouting, or saying crazy things, though they usually end up making a fool of themselves. And nobody likes that, which is one reason why the ICE-COLD GLARE works so well in front of innocent bystanders. Consider what would have happened in the last example if this dialogue had taken place during class. The teacher comes across in control, not the student, who ends up looking like a brat.

Silence Exercises

As I mentioned above, SILENCE tactics are simple to use but hard to master. And that's where practice comes in. (I'll have more to say about practicing psychological self-defense in Chapter 11.) For now, here are some exercises to help you master SILENCE, the STARE, and the ICE-COLD GLARE:

1. This first exercise requires a practice partner (e.g., spouse or housemate). Your partner bombards you with questions, which you silently ignore. It's hard at first, because your inclination is to make some response or gesture to acknowledge your partner. Resist the temptation! Instead, completely ignore him or her until you can do it without feeling uncomfortable. You can even have him or her plead with you to answer or throw increasingly hostile comments your way, while you continue to ignore him or her and remain silent. Again, this is a hard exercise, but it can also be a lot of fun once you get into the swing of it. In fact, the more difficult your partner makes it on you during practice, the better prepared you will be to use SILENCE in real life situations.

2. This second exercise also requires a practice partner. In this one, you both sit facing each other, and remain totally silent for as long as possible. The idea is to use SILENCE and the STARE, without becoming uncomfortable or cracking up. (Yes, most people find it hard not to laugh when they first practice this exercise.) Try to work up to staring at each other for five minutes at a time without looking away or laughing.

3. Practice glaring at yourself in a mirror. Get the look you think is the most intimidating, remembering what it feels like so you can later recapture the facial expression without a mirror. You may want to check out the cold, glaring expressions of the actors in various "Spaghetti Westerns" for some ideas on what killer glares look like. Then try using the ICE-COLD GLARE with your partner, as in exercise number two above.

4. In this one, your partner throws every insult, hostile jab, and command that he or she can at you, while you practice SILENCE, the STARE, and the ICE-COLD GLARE. Your partner should show no mercy. Remember, the more you practice these tactics, the more fun they are to practice, and the more adept you'll be at applying them in your life.

5. Exercises with a partner are very important, but your practice doesn't stop there. The next step is to *generalize* your newly acquired skills to situations in the "real world." Try using SILENCE in various public settings, such as in a grocery checkout line or in the drive-through at your bank. However, remember that SILENCE doesn't imply being mean to "innocents" (then you're no better than your opponents). You can just as easily smile at the store clerk as frown, all the while not saying anything. The idea is for you to get used to not responding to strangers, while at the same time noting that nothing *terrible* happens as a result.

Chapter 10

Nasty Opponents

Lovers and madmen have such seething brains,
Such shaping fantasies, that apprehend
More than cool reason ever comprehends.
— William Shakespeare

When under fire from opponents, it can seem like you're up against "madmen with seething brains." Therefore, I'm devoting this chapter to describing the personality types of those nasty opponents you're most likely to encounter in everyday life. Having a better understanding of your opponents' psyches and motives gives you "more than cool reason"; it gives you additional cognitive ammo with which to protect yourself.

In case you're wondering, personality characteristics tend to be deeply ingrained and not easily changeable (except perhaps after years of psychotherapy, and even then there's no guarantee). That's why I suggest you use Self-Defense Responses to deal with nasty opponents, rather than letting insults slide or expecting your opponents to change somehow. I hope the following brief descriptions will provide you with some insights into these characters' typical methods.

So without further delay, I'd like to introduce you to 25 of the most common varieties of nasty opponents. (Unfortunately, there are more than 25; opponents tend to be a diverse bunch.)

1. **The Criticizer.** This opponent is fond of pointing out your imperfections. To him or her, your entire person is seriously flawed. Everything you do is bad. All of your feelings, hopes, and dreams are wrong. And the Criticizer feels compelled to tell you all about it, even if you don't want to hear it. Like so many opponents, the Criticizer is typically motivated by low self-esteem, deep-seated hostility, and an irrational need to feel powerful.

2. **The Anal-Retentive (or Perfectionist).** This character demands that everyone and everything in the universe be clean, in order, and without flaw of any kind. Perfection is the absolute norm here. Because the Anal-Retentive is obsessional about details, he usually can't rest unless everything is in its proper place. The Anal-Retentive may choose to live alone so he can better control his living space.

3. **The Value-Pusher (or Proselytizer).** The Value-Pusher insists that you share his beliefs, values, and life interests. There's usually no middle ground with the Value-Pusher. His way is the only way. And because he can't tolerate being around people with different perspectives about life, he pulls every trick in the book to convince them that he's right and they're wrong. That's why religion, politics, and feminism are taboo topics when you're with the Value-Pusher.

4. **The Button-Pusher.** As his name implies, this one knows just how to get a rise out of you. The Button-Pusher can easily pick out your weak spots, and then turn these against you. His primary purpose is to exert control by stirring up disputes and making others miserable, which he does by carefully playing on your sensitivities.

5. **The Guilterizer.** The Guilterizer uses guilt to manipulate. "Shame on you!" "What would your mother say?" and "You're a disgrace to this company" are examples of the kind of lines the Guilterizer uses to convince you of your worthlessness and trick you into doing what he or she wants. Relatives are often notorious for pulling this kind of stuff.

6. **The Egotist (or Invalidator).** The Egotist is "full of himself," so to speak. This type is arrogant; has a grandiose sense of self-importance; feels brilliant, beautiful, and successful; expects special

consideration and treatment; turns every conversation back to himself; brags about talents and achievements; is constantly fishing for compliments; and is bent on making you feel inferior or incompetent. His typical *modus operandi* is to set you up, get you to disclose or talk about what you believe are your positive traits, personal strengths and accomplishments, and then invalidate everything you just said. In this way, the Egotist overcompensates for personal feelings of inadequacy and envy.

7. **The Intimidator.** A type of Egotist, this opponent sets out to intimidate others. His inflated sense of ego demands that he "push his weight around," taking advantage of others to achieve his own ends. This opponent intimidates people to overcompensate for feelings of inferiority, although it may seem like he does it simply "for kicks."

8. **The Name-Dropper (or One-Upper).** Another type of Egotist, the Name-Dropper likes to show you how important he is by letting you know he's best friends with loads of very important people. This one also likes to "One-Up" anything you say in an attempt to show you he's smarter and richer than you could ever be, but at the same time has had more problems than you could ever know.

9. **The Charmer.** Beware, this "con artist" can sweet talk you into anything! He appears perfectly sincere, honest, legitimate, and trustworthy. Yet his ultimate goal is to manipulate you, usually by showering you with flattery, adulation, praise, kindness, and thoughtfulness (including expensive gifts). Nothing is too costly to achieve his ends. "Killing them with kindness" is the Charmer's motto.

10. **The Passive-Aggressor.** Another "con artist," the Passive-Aggressor's strategy is to tell you one thing (usually what you want to hear), all the while he thinks or does something entirely different. He does this to avoid being accountable. You never know where you stand with the Passive-Aggressor.

11. **The Accuser (or Blamer).** The Accuser is a "Pass-The-Buck" type of opponent. He or she is constantly shifting blame to others. The primary motive here is to avoid responsibility for one's

choices and actions. And what better way to do this than to find a scapegoat!

12. **The Complainer (or Griper).** This one never has anything good to say. He's always griping about something. The Complainer is definitely a negative person. Because nobody can stand to sit and listen to it for long, people usually run in the opposite direction when they see the Complainer coming.

13. **The Power-Monger (or Tyrant).** This controlling individual is obsessed with dominating others and telling them how to run their lives. There's no room for compromise with the Power-Monger. It's his way — period! The basic motive underlying the Power-Monger's style is fear of losing control, which for him spells total failure as a person.

14. **The Hawk.** Ever heard the expression, "Watching them like a hawk"? That's exactly what this opponent does. A type of Power-Monger, the Hawk is preoccupied with monitoring everything everybody else says and does. He or she remains hypervigilant to details, as well as the possibility that someone might try to "pull a fast one." Like the Power-Monger, the Hawk fears losing control.

15. **The Squasher.** The Squasher is interested in only one thing — getting what he wants, regardless of the cost. This one doesn't hesitate for a minute to lie, cheat, steal, insult, abuse, malign — whatever it takes. Competitive coworkers often fall into this category.

16. **The Pressurizer.** This one achieves his ends by pressuring you until you cave in. Unfortunately, the more you resist, the more of a challenge you become. Pushy salespeople are notorious for this sort of thing.

17. **The Exploiter.** The Exploiter is an expert at reading other people, identifying the "nice" nonassertive ones, and then talking them into doing things that aren't in their best interest. He has a fascinating, unique ability to manipulate others, while at the same time making his rationale for "needing a little extra" seem perfectly reasonable.

18. **The Penny-Pincher (or Tightwad).** This miserly character expects everything for nothing. He wants others to perform at top

efficiency, but doesn't want to give them adequate support. Saving money is the Penny-Pincher's primary concern.

19. **The Screamer.** The Screamer is the one who gets his or her way by shouting, yelling, roaring, hollering, bellowing, crying, screaming, wailing, whooping, yammering, or shrieking (or all of these together!). People quickly do anything necessary to quiet this character. No one wants to listen to the Screamer, especially in public, and he or she knows it. The Screamer is a type of Intimidator.

20. **The Bunny Boiler (or Borderline).** This "Fatal Attraction" type will do almost anything to get attention and manipulate you. For instance, he may call you at all hours of the day and night, send you annoying letters, leave 57 messages before you've arrived at work, show up on your doorstep at 5:45 a.m. or 11:45 p.m., or even threaten or attempt suicide (blaming you, of course). Again, these are all attempts to coax you into doing his will. The scary part about the Bunny Boiler is that he can seem perfectly rational, that is, until you cross wires with him.

21. **The Hysteric (or Sh**-Stirrer).** The Hysteric loves to stir it up and create commotion. Why? Because it's entertaining! He or she loves to get everybody in an uproar, and then sit back and enjoy the fireworks. The hysteric loves drama and tragedy; rapidly shifts mood; frequently overreacts; needs constant attention; requires others' praise and approval; has little or no frustration tolerance; and may even be seductive in everyday dealings.

22. **The Savior.** The Savior feels compelled to play the role of the martyr, make personal sacrifices, rescue others, and fix things. The Savior wears a halo that says, "Call me for help."

23. **The Joker.** This individual is always cutting other people down, but in a joking way. His remarks are seemingly harmless and funny, although the true motive behind his "kidding" is to hurt you. The fact that he delivers assaults in a joshing manner is irrelevant. The Joker is typically driven by anger and/or insecurity.

24. **The Dead Fish.** The Dead Fish opponent literally has no personality. There's nothing pleasant or fun about this person. He or she rates a double zero on a 10-point happy scale. The Dead Fish controls you by boring you to death.

25. **The Whopper.** This "deluxe combo" opponent has the personality characteristics of at least two of the above opponents.

No doubt, some of these characters can be pretty ferocious. That's why throughout *Don't Let Them Psych You Out!* I've likened dealing with difficult people to doing battle, which is what confrontations feel like to many people. That's also why I decided to devote this chapter to describing opponents' different personality styles. Understanding what you're up against really helps when it comes to handling threats and conflicts.

Confrontations involve much more than personalities, though. They involve *people.* (Yes, opponents are people, too.) Surely you've discovered by now that opponents come in a variety of shapes and sizes. Some take the form of driving bosses, others meddling relatives, and still others possessive friends, to name but a few. So my point here? Insight into others is important. Very important. But so is insight into yourself. You can't expect to understand your opponent if you don't first understand yourself.

Of course, insight isn't the entire answer, either. You can't expect to overcome personal (and impersonal) attacks if you aren't willing to think things through *and* work things out. Recognizing opponents' styles and patterns, as well as your own for dealing with them, is only a first step to developing a psychological self-defense strategy that will work for you. Specifically, you need to carefully consider where you and your opponent are coming from, weigh your options, decide what you're going to do to remedy an uncomfortable situation, and then follow through with your plan. Simply stated, knowledge and insight are only two pieces of the puzzle; it's through personal *action* that you empower yourself. Or as the French philosopher Henri Bergson so aptly put it, "Think like a man of action, act like a man of thought."

Chapter 11

Preparing for Battle

Be prepared.

— **Boy Scout Motto**

Do any of these remarks sound familiar?

"Whenever a disagreement comes up, my heart starts racing, I end up choking on my words, and then I feel like a real loser."
"Just knowing that I need to confront one of my employees about their work is enough to send me to bed for a week."
"I'm totally stressed out for days when I know I have to return an item for a refund. Sometimes I get so upset that I just forget about the whole thing."

If you can relate to any of the above, then you know what I mean when I say that *interpersonal conflicts are stressful.* Although some opponents actually thrive on conflicts, most people (especially meek and shy types) do their best to avoid stressful disagreements and power plays. One reason for this is that people generally don't like the uncomfortable physical feelings of stress (e.g., racing heart, lump in the throat, choking sensations, stomach and intestinal disturbances, faint feelings). Another reason is that people know they can't think as clearly when they're nervous or stressed out.

Is there any way to minimize the stressful nature of conflicts? Can the unpleasant physical symptoms brought on by an impending dispute be avoided? Is it possible to reduce the likelihood of blanking out and inadvertently handing over the keys to your life? Absolutely, *by preparing yourself beforehand to meet difficult people and situations!* You learn to expect the unexpected. You take time to "center" yourself before problematic encounters. And like a good Scout, you think and plan ahead. In other words, "preparing" yourself entails 1) keeping alert, 2) learning to relax, and 3) practicing self-defense skills until they become second nature. You can virtually "inoculate" yourself against stress when you do these three simple things.

It Pays to Be Paranoid!

Sometimes it really does pay to be paranoid. By "paranoid," I don't mean having a mental disorder; I mean remaining alert to the possibility that a conflict may be just around the corner. Before you get out of bed in the morning, walk out the door, or answer the phone, remind yourself that there's potential for conflict in every interaction. Then you're continually ready to deal with whatever problems might arise during your day.

I've frequently affirmed the value of keeping alert to potential conflicts in my own life. I remember some years ago during training when, fairly exhausted from a heavy therapy schedule, I let it slip to my clinic director that I was also interested in the teaching and writing side of psychology and not just the clinical side. Big mistake! The prevailing ethic at this clinic was to perform direct service, not write or teach, so my comment was in direct conflict with the status quo. Fortunately, the situation straightened itself out in a matter of weeks. I learned a very valuable lesson from this early career experience: always be alert and careful about what you say and to whom you say it.

Learning to Relax

Learning to relax is probably the single most valuable technique you can master to prepare ahead for difficult encounters. By now you know that the best time to think your way out of a conflict is when you're calm and collected. It's the wise person, then, who learns to relax *before* trying to take on the world.

We've all read about people who meditate, repeat mantras, or practice yoga to evoke altered states of consciousness and deep levels of relaxation. Scientists now know what the "mystics" have known for centuries — that relaxation is physically and emotionally beneficial and can be learned. What you may not know is that you don't have to move to Tibet and study with a lama to master relaxation. You can learn it right in the comfort of your home. (For example, there are many self-relaxation tapes and instruction booklets available commercially.)

One of the most widely practiced systems of relaxation training is *progressive relaxation* (PR) (Jacobson, 1970). During PR, the individual sits quietly in a comfortable chair and listens to a therapist or tape directing him or her to tense and relax each of the major muscle systems of the body. Practicing PR reduces the person's overall levels of stress and helps him or her feel relaxed more of the time, often in just a few weeks.

Another system of relaxation training involves eliciting the *relaxation response*. After years of studying meditation and other relaxation techniques, cardiologist Herbert Benson concluded that long, drawn-out, complicated methods aren't necessary to learn relaxation. He then developed the following straightforward procedure for inducing calm, outlined in his book *The Relaxation Response* (Benson, 1992, pp. 162-163):

1. Sit quietly in a comfortable position.
2. Close your eyes.
3. Deeply relax all of your muscles, beginning at your feet and progressing up to your face. Keep them relaxed.
4. Breathe through your nose. Become aware of your breathing. As you breathe out, say the word, "ONE," silently to yourself. For example, breathe IN...OUT, "ONE"; IN...OUT, "ONE"; etc. Breathe easily and naturally.
5. Continue for 10 to 20 minutes. You may open your eyes to check the time, but do not use an alarm. When you finish, sit quietly for several minutes, at first with your eyes closed and later with your eyes opened. Do not stand up for a few minutes.

6. Do not worry about whether you are successful in achieving a deep level of relaxation. Maintain a passive attitude and permit relaxation to occur at its own pace. When distracting thoughts occur, try to ignore them by not dwelling upon them and return to repeating "ONE." With practice, the response should come with little effort. Practice the technique once or twice daily, but not within two hours after any meal, since the digestive processes seem to interfere with the elicitation of the Relaxation Response.

In addition to relaxing prior to facing your opponent, you may find it helpful to use CALMING STATEMENTS whenever you feel an attack of nerves coming on. Ideally you want your body to associate the pleasant sensations of relaxation with your CALMING STATEMENTS. So you should practice them during or immediately following your relaxation exercises, while you're still relaxed. That way, you'll eventually be able to bring about instant relaxation "on command." I use the following CALMING STATEMENTS (said either out loud or to myself) to relax myself both *before* and *during* stressful situations:

"Keep calm."
"Stay relaxed."
"Be centered."
"Keep it together."
"Don't be nervous."
"Don't lose it."
"I'm in control."
"This isn't worth getting upset about."

You may also want to try taking a TIME-OUT during times of stress. During a TIME-OUT, you remove yourself from a volatile situation in order to relax and gather your thoughts. Taking a TIME-OUT can help you avoid having the kind of emotional outburst that you might later regret.

Practice Makes Imperfect!

"Practice makes *im*perfect?" you ask? Exactly! "Why *im*perfect?" Because your goal isn't just to learn assertiveness, but also to accept that you're an imperfect, fallible human being. And the best way to do this is to *practice, practice, practice* the techniques and strategies outlined in ***Don't Let Them Psych You Out!*** Then you're prepared to handle your opponents, while also maintaining a rational attitude about conflicts and what you can or can't do about them.

Have you ever noticed how when you begin practicing something it feels awkward, but with time, patience, and practice the activity gets easier and easier? Why? Because when you practice a certain activity, you effectively train it into your nervous system. My favorite example of this is learning to play the piano. When you first try to play, it feels strange to the touch. To say the least, coordinating your hands (i.e., one hand playing the melody, the other harmony), using the foot pedals, and reading music — while trying to sound musical and not hit wrong notes — is difficult and can be very discouraging. However, after many, many hours of practice, playing the piano becomes much more automatic, until one day you can sit and make music without having to think about it.

Another good example of the importance of practice is learning martial arts. At first, the body stances, blocks, punches, and kicks feel unnatural and awkward. These moves require considerable conscious thought and effort to execute. But with practice, they become so automatic that the individual doesn't need to think at all about which moves to use when and where.

It should now be clear why you need to practice the various responses and strategies outlined in this book. Once you've practiced and trained your nervous system for psychological self-defense, you won't have to think about the techniques in order to use them. They'll be an automatic reflex, available for immediate use whenever danger threatens.

So what's the best way to practice? The answer is deceptively simple — *often, consistently,* and *in real life!* For your practice to take hold, it should be done on a regular, preferably daily, basis. You should also practice in real life situations, as well as at home with a partner. Just because you can successfully use a particular defense tactic during practice doesn't mean you can do the same during a real conflict. True change, then, occurs only when you *generalize* your skills from the "practice room" to the "concert hall." In other words, the more you practice your psychological self-defense skills both at home and *in vivo,* the easier it'll be for you to employ them in every-day encounters. (The procedure for mastering SILENCE detailed at the end of Chapter 9 is a good example of how to practice and generalize the various self-defense tactics described in *Don't Let Them Psych You Out!*.)

Part II
When You Psych Yourself Out

Chapter 12
Conquering
Worry and Anxiety

Archie doesn't know how to worry without getting upset.
— **Edith Bunker**

Scientific research has recently brought to light many facts about worry and anxiety, including:

- Between 5% and 10% of the general population have one or more *phobias.*
- Some 35% of the general population has had at least one *panic attack* during the previous year.
- More people *worry* about speaking in public than being killed in a nuclear war.
- The number of people suffering from *anxiety disorders* is greater than that of any other mental disorder, including addiction and depression.

Without a doubt, anxiety — the irrational fear of people, places, and things, especially of what *might happen* in the future — is one of, if not *the,* most defeating emotions people experience. By "irrational fear," I mean fear that goes beyond what most people would consider normal, or "rational." For example, it's rational to fear walking down dark alleys at night; it's irrational to fear leaving your home because "there might be criminals lurking out there somewhere."

Although in more severe cases anxiety may take the form of a *bona fide* anxiety disorder (e.g., phobias; panic disorder; generalized anxiety), a far greater number of people experience any of a multitude of daily worries and anxieties. Consider for a moment the kinds of things that you worry about. Finances? Inflation? Potential unemployment? Bad credit? In-laws? Kids? Divorce? Crime? Health? Confrontations at school? Not having anything to worry about? If you're like most people, the list goes on and on.

Not only does worry involve "vague" fears like not having enough money; it can involve specific ones, too. Anxiety is sometimes directly associated with, or provoked by, a particular individual, group of individuals, or situation. For example, you may be terrified of your boss, afraid of your students *en masse,* or scared to address the PTA. Irrational and excessive fears of specific people, places, and things are called *phobias.*

So why do you worry about things? Could it be you believe that by worrying you can somehow control the future and prevent negative events from occurring? This is actually the case with many worriers. Because their fears consistently fail to materialize (being highly improbable of occurring in the first place), they mistakenly conclude that their worrying is responsible for saving the day. More simply put, worriers claim a "cause and effect" relationship that isn't there.

Have you ever considered the possibility that most of what you worry about is actually out of your hands? Think about it for a minute. Worry and anxiety are future-oriented. Their essence is the *what if* Crazy-Maker (CM):

- What if I lose my job?
- What if my kids start taking drugs?
- What if I get sick?

What if...?, What if...?, What if...?

And these *what ifs* are nothing more than absolutistic musturbating, demanding, and catastrophizing in disguise:

- I *must* keep my job. It would be *terrible* if I lost my job.

- I *demand* assurance that my kids will always do what I want them to. It would *awful* if they didn't.
- I *must* stay well. It would be *horrible* if I couldn't tolerate the discomfort of being sick.

I must...!, I demand...!, I must...!
It's terrible...!, It's awful...!, It's horrible...!

It'd be great if we humans could control our destiny with the degree of certainty that the worrier demands. Alas, life isn't so easy. In fact, you have very little control over what happens to you next year, next week, or even tomorrow. You can do a superb job at work, and still get fired. You can teach your children how to say NO to drugs, and still watch them succumb. You can exercise, eat right, and watch your weight, and still get sick. Just because you do all the "right" things doesn't *assure* that you'll be free of problems. You can work to minimize your risks (which is certainly worthwhile), but there's no *guarantee* things will be the way you want.

I don't want to imply that you shouldn't think or be concerned about your finances, job, or kids, or that you shouldn't try to work out your problems. Quite to the contrary. There's nothing wrong with being *interested* in or *concerned* about the future. It's being *anxious* about it that creates hardships. When you're concerned about something, you're focused on the present, and thus free to take charge and rationally act against negative influences. But when you're anxious about something, you're focused on the future, and thus paralyzed. So rather than acting to improve your life, you end up wallowing in a pool of irrationality.

"Wouldn't it just be easier for me to give up and forget about trying to tackle my problems?" Maybe in the short run, but never in the long run! Anyone can quit. It's the easy way out.

Acting on your own behalf, however, is what psychological self-defense is all about. To this end, I offer you some of the same techniques for overcoming worry that I teach to my anxious clients and students:

1. Make that all-important decision to change. Yes, friend, the ball's in your court, not mine or someone else's. It's only when *you* choose to quit worrying that you'll be able to quit.

2. Be sure to keep a realistic, rational attitude about what you can and can't do once you decide to change. Too many people start a program, overdo it, burn out, never finish the program, and then get down on themselves (or their therapist) for "failing." I can't tell you how many times clients have told me something to the effect, "Therapy doesn't work. I tried it for two days and nothing happened. I'm still nervous!" I'm quick to remind them that because their problems didn't develop overnight, it'll probably take longer than two days for therapy to help.

3. Use cognitive reframing to alter your assumptions of *having* to control the future, or *demanding* a guarantee that everything go your way. This means identifying, disputing, and countering your CMs, including all of your *what ifs* and *musts*. For example, here's a sample Dispute and Sensible Reply (SR) for our first *must* above:

   • Who says that I *must* keep my job? And why would it be *terrible* if I lost my job? (Dispute)
   • It's *nice,* not a must, to keep my job. And it would only be *inconvenient*, not terrible, if I lost it. (SR)

4. Have handy a list of READY REPLIES (RRs) to use when opponents try to make you anxious. Unfortunately, there are opponents who love to frighten people whom they think are weaker than themselves. The Intimidator is notorious for this sort of thing, doing his best to scare you into doing what he wants. Following are a few of the RRs that I find helpful for dealing with Intimidators and other types of opponents:

   "Hmmm."
   "I don't understand."
   "I'm not sure."
   "What?"
   "Really?"

   Deliberate SILENCE is also excellent for this purpose.

5. Develop a plan for dealing with anxiety-provoking encounters. One way to do this is through use of relaxation exercises and CALMING STATEMENTS to counter anxiety and induce calm.

Another way is through *systematic desensitization*, in which you gradually approach the people and situations that frighten you. Here's how it works:

a.   Devise an *anxiety hierarchy* of situations that trigger anxiety, from the least (at the bottom of the list) to the most frightening (at the top of the list) for any given scenario. An anxiety hierarchy for fear of public speaking might look something like this in ascending order of intensity):

10) Accepting an invitation to give a speech to a large crowd. (the least anxiety-provoking scenario)
9)   Thinking about giving a speech to a large crowd.
8)   Preparing a speech at home.
7)   Preparing to leave home before practicing and giving a speech.
6)   Entering an empty auditorium to practice giving a speech.
5)   Practicing giving a speech in an empty auditorium.
4)   Waiting in the rear of a crowded auditorium before walking to the podium.
3)   Walking to the podium in front of a large crowd.
2)   Standing in front of a large crowd.
1)   Giving a speech to a large crowd. (the most anxiety-provoking scenario)

b.   After becoming relaxed, imagine yourself overcoming your fears. You do this by gradually moving up your anxiety hierarchy, beginning with the least anxiety-provoking item, and remaining relaxed at all times. Should you become nervous at any time during the procedure, you return to the previous item on the list until the anxiety passes, after which you continue moving up your hierarchy.

c.   Once you can successfully do this, it's time to face these same fears *in vivo*. In other words, the procedure is the same as b. above, except this time you do it by moving up your hierarchy "in person."

6.   Unfortunately, when faced with a person or situation that provokes anxiety or worry (e.g., an impending quarrel), almost everybody does the worst thing possible. Instead of facing their

fears, they <u>avoid</u> them. Why is this so bad? Because it's quite clear from psychological research that avoiding an anxiety-provoking encounter reinforces the anxiety response. That is, the anxiety becomes increasingly worse each time you avoid the person or situation. The bottom line here is that you can't expect to conquer your fears and worries until you're willing to confront them. And the longer you avoid them, the harder this will be to do.

7. Last but not least, *practice, practice, practice!*

COGNITIVE REFRAMING CHART
("Worry")

Situation:

Crazy-Maker:
Dispute:
Sensible Reply:

Situation:

Crazy-Maker:
Dispute:
Sensible Reply:

Situation:

Crazy-Maker:
Dispute:
Sensible Reply:

Situation:

Crazy-Maker:
Dispute:
Sensible Reply:

Chapter 13

Keep Your Cool!

A hot-tempered man stirs up strife,
But the slow to anger pacifies contention.
— Proverbs 15:18

We've all said, heard, and even believed irrationalities like:

"So-and-so *makes* me so mad!"
"It's his *fault,* not mine!"
"This or that *gets* me so angry!"

For most of us, there seems to be a cosmic "cause and effect" relationship out there controlling everything. Event A supposedly causes Thought B and Feeling C. Granted, and as we've noted in other chapters, events, thoughts, and feelings do influence each other. But do events *cause* thoughts or feelings? Absolutely not!

The major premise of ***Don't Let Them Psych You Out!*** is that it's our perceptions of events that determine our feelings and reactions, not the events themselves. Yes, you're ultimately in charge of your thoughts, emotions, and behaviors. It may feel like someone else is, or you might want to shift the blame to someone else, but your life really is your own responsibility. And nowhere is this principle more apparent than with anger. Thus, your boss doesn't *make* you mad. You *choose* to be mad. It's not your spouse's *fault* that you're miserable. You *choose* to be miserable. The broken dishwasher doesn't *get* you angry. You *choose* to be angry.

How do anger reactions happen in the first place? Applying our "Event-Belief-Reaction" model (Chapter 2) to anger, we see that anger reactions follow a fairly typical pattern, breaking down into four basic steps:

1. A particular event occurs in the environment.
2. You perceive the event as an "anger trigger."
3. You experience the emotion of anger.
4. You decide to express, or not express, your anger.

According to this model, an event occurs in the environment ("event") that the person perceives as something that *should* make him angry ("thought"). Then the person feels angry ("emotion") and is faced with deciding whether or not to express the anger ("behavior"). It's clear that all four steps in an anger reaction are related, but it's a leap of illogic to conclude that one or more of these steps *causes* the others.

What does this have to do with learning to keep your cool? You can avoid having an anger reaction (i.e., avoid reaching Steps #3 and #4) by intervening at the thinking step of this model (i.e., Step #2). In reality, there's usually little or nothing you can do to prevent Step #1 from occurring, as life gives us plenty of opportunities to lose it (some of these being justifiable, of course). But there's a great deal you can do at Step #2 to avoid moving on to Steps #3 and #4. In other words, you can change how you think about your potential anger triggers. You can see them for what they are — nuisances and annoyances that aren't worth getting upset about. And because it's only *unfortunate* and not *terrible* when such negatives happen, you don't *have* to react to them with hostility, even though this may be your initial impulse.

Here's an example. Let's say that an obnoxious coworker starts making ugly remarks about your family. What happens? First, there are the remarks your opponent makes (Step #1). Then, you hear the remarks and perceive them as hostile assaults, which you don't like (Step #2). As a result, you feel a rise of anger as your "blood starts to boil" (Step #3). And finally, you decide that your opponent's remarks deserve retribution, so you shout and/or belt him one in the face (Step #4).

Who's in control of your reactions in a case like this? Your opponent? It may feel that way (and he wants you to believe that!), but he's not. You are! Whether or not you allow malicious remarks or the like to get under your skin *is entirely up to you.* You don't *have* to feel angry or come out fighting. There's no one *twisting your arm* to lose your cool.

At the heart of reacting to various events or "triggers" with anger are two absolutistic *musts:*

1. I *must* get what I want, when I want it, or else life is *terrible.*
2. People who don't do what I want are bad, and they *must* be punished.

These can take the form of such demanding sorts of nonsense as:

- He should call me more often. What a creep!
- She should have spent more money on my birthday present. How thoughtless!
- Why don't you pay more attention to me, like so-and-so does his girlfriend?
- The car must never break down or need repairs.
- The dog had better not wet on the carpet again, or he's history!
- If the gadget doesn't start working like it's supposed to soon, I'm going to break it in half and throw it out.
- What a terrible thing to say!
- You'd better shape up, or else!

Any of these ring a bell? You bet they do! People engage in ridiculous self-talk like this all of the time. And what's the common factor here? That's right, those irrational, unrealistic beliefs of *demandingness.* Just about anytime you feel hostile or angry, you can trace it back to your self-defeating *musts, shoulds, needs, haves,* and *oughts,* which we've been unmasking throughout this book. And how do you get rid of these? Like I've said many times before, by disputing your Crazy-Makers and replacing them with Sensible Replies. This is how to deal with the *thinking* part of anger.

"From all of this, it sounds like anger is a bad emotion?" No, not at all. I want to be clear here that anger, *per se,* isn't wicked or evil. It's a normal human emotion. It's a built-in mechanism for expressing your dislikes and protecting yourself and loved ones from verbal, physical, or mental assault. Anger is even beneficial to relationships and conflicts, helping people clarify their commitments, effectively solve problems, and clear the air.

Now we come to dealing with the *saying* and *doing* parts of anger (Warren & Zgourides, 1991). Basically, there are two ways to handle and express this emotion. The first type, *destructive* ("inappropriate") expression of anger, is what leads to problems for most people. Destructive anger is the explosive, impulsive, and uncontrolled type of anger that alienates others and impedes rather than facilitates problem-solving. This anger reaction is frequently the result of poor or absent communication, causing the "Chip-On-The-Shoulder" effect for all parties. As interpersonal issues are ignored, the chips pile higher on people's shoulders, and it gets easier to knock them off and start a fight. An example of this is the husband who is angry at his wife for not paying attention to him, but instead of addressing that issue blows up at her for squeezing the toothpaste from the "wrong" end of the tube. Because of this "Chip-On-The-Shoulder" effect, couples' quarrels almost always start over insignificant issues, rather than real ones.

I'm reminded of a situation that happened to me a few years back. As an author, I send out a number of book proposals each year to locate publishers for whatever projects I'm interested in at the time. On one occasion, I approached a large publishing house about my doing a textbook for them, and they graciously agreed to send out my proposal to several psychology reviewers around the country. (This is common practice; textbook publishers generally like to obtain feedback from experts in the field, to see if a project is viable and marketable, before offering an author a contract.)

Well, the first of the three reviews was excellent, and the second was okay. But then the third review arrived. It was the most malicious, insulting piece of garbage I'd ever received (and I've received many, many reviews over the years). Reviewer #3 attacked me personally, claimed psychologists like myself who work with disadvantaged populations only required "an 11th grade education" (the reviewer's own words!), accused me of not knowing anything about my speciality, etc., etc., etc. To make matters worse, the review was hand-written, presumably because I didn't deserve a typed one. I couldn't believe it. I was so angry. "How dare that reviewer insult me like that!" I thought. "And how dare a publisher send me such an insulting review!"

The more I thought about the whole thing, the more furious I became. I really let this goofball get to me! In a fit of anger, I decided to return the favor, and I wrote back an extremely nasty letter (rivaling the reviewer's letter) to the editor, asking her to forward my "feedback" to Reviewer #3. Regrettably, my letter was so biting that the publisher refused to forward it for fear of upsetting the reviewer. (I wish she and the reviewer had been as considerate of my feelings!)

Looking back, in the short run, it felt great to write that letter, but in the long run it served no purpose. If I'd calmly written an objective, rational response to the obnoxious reviewer, then perhaps my letter might have found its way to him. Instead, I let my anger get the best of me. Fortunately, the experience was not a total loss, as I learned a number of valuable lessons: 1) never underestimate the power of letters; 2) write, but wait and reread potentially upsetting letters before mailing them; and 3) be thick-skinned (i.e., alter my perceptions) when it comes to what others write, say, think, and do.

At this point it should be apparent that the most effective means of handling your anger is through its *constructive* ("appropriate") expression. Constructive anger is the patient, thought-out, and controlled type of anger that demonstrates respect for others and facilitates problem-solving. Here are a few ideas for you:

1. When faced with an anger trigger, it's often helpful to take a TIME-OUT before doing or saying anything. During a TIME-OUT, you physically remove yourself from a potentially volatile situation, allowing yourself some space to cool off, clear your head, and think through your available options. It can be as easy as this:

Jack: You know, I detest everything you stand for. You're a liberal, feminist do-gooder who'd love to see our country go down the drain.

Jill: Before I say something I'll regret, I'm going to take a TIME-OUT.

If for some reason you can't physically leave the situation, mentally leave, even if just for a few seconds. Some people silently count to 10 before responding. Others look away from or STARE at the opponent. Still others close their eyes and try to distract themselves. Do whatever works best for you.

Jack: I said you're a liberal, feminist do-gooder who'd love to see our country go down the drain.

Jill: (keeping silent, counting to 10, looking away) (SILENCE; TIME-OUT)

Jack: Don't you have anything to say?

Jill: (still silent, counting, looking away) (SILENCE; TIME-OUT)

Jack: Well?

Jill: (getting herself together; quietly responding). You sound really hostile right now. I'd prefer to talk about this later when we're both up to it. (NEGATIVE VOCAL TRACKING; PROCESS COMMENT; PREFERENCE STATEMENT)

By taking a second or two to gather her senses before quietly responding, Jill diffuses a stressful situation and avoids a quarrel with Jack (or at least postpones it until *she's* ready).

2. When on the receiving end of someone else's anger, avoid becoming defensive. Don't retaliate. Instead, use good listening skills — POSITIVE EYE CONTACT, OPEN BODY POSTURE, ENCOURAGING GESTURES, and PARAPHRASING — to let the person know you're listening, and DETAILING to obtain more specific information about the upset. This is especially important if the other person is someone whose feelings you genuinely care about (e.g., your spouse).

Bob: (watching television) Honey, want to get me a beer?
Carol: Get your own damn beer! All you ever do is drink beer and watch football. I'm sick of it!
Bob: It sounds like you're upset about my spending so much time watching football. Is that what's bothering you, Carol? Or is it something else? (PARAPHRASING; DETAILING)

3. Remember, it never hurts to show some respect for the other person, even if you disagree with or dislike him. This means accepting the other person's right to be angry, as well as freely acknowledging *your* role in his anger reaction. (Yes, these things are rarely one-sided.) Further, don't be afraid or too proud to apologize if you decide you're in the wrong. Continuing with our example:

Carol: Yes and no. I'm just tired and cranky tonight. I guess what I'm saying is I'd like a little more attention from you when I'm feeling stressed out.
Bob: I don't blame you. Sometimes I really get preoccupied with the game. I apologize. How about I give you a nice backrub when the game's over?
Carol: Sounds wonderful. Sorry about swearing at you. How about I get you that beer?
Bob: Great! Thanks.

4. What can be done when an individual is getting on *your* nerves? If you want to call the situation to his or her attention, use BEHAVIOR STATEMENTS to identify specific behaviors that bother you, rather than overgeneralizing.

Ted: You know, sweetheart, I have something I'd like to say.
Alice: What's that?
Ted: You're a dirty, filthy, stinking slob. (overgeneralizing)

versus

Ted: I'd prefer it if you didn't leave your panty hose in the bathroom sink. (PREFERENCE STATEMENT; BEHAVIOR STATEMENT)

It doesn't take much imagination to figure out which of Ted's responses will start a fight, and which will facilitate some quality dialogue and problem-solving.

5. Finally, there may be times when someone expresses anger not *at* you, but *to* you, as a sort of sounding board. The most common response, though notoriously wrong, is to tell the person something to the effect, "You shouldn't let stuff like that bother you." This is often taken as criticism. As a sounding board, it's much more helpful to use good listening skills. After all, the person wants you to listen. If he also wants your advice, he'll ask for it.

COGNITIVE REFRAMING CHART
("Anger")

Situation:

Crazy-Maker:
Dispute:
Sensible Reply:

Situation:

Crazy-Maker:
Dispute:
Sensible Reply:

Situation:

Crazy-Maker:
Dispute:
Sensible Reply:

Situation:

Crazy-Maker:
Dispute:
Sensible Reply:

Chapter 14
Learning to Handle
Friendly Criticism

I love criticism just so long as it's unqualified praise.
— **Noel Coward**

Few people love criticism, especially when it seems that the other person's intent is to hurt or manipulate. But like so many of the potential negatives described in ***Don't Let Them Psych You Out!***, it's not the intent or nature of the criticism that makes the difference, it's how you interpret and accept it. In other words, you can view criticism as a threat to your self-worth and fold under the pressure (which is probably what the other guy wants you to do), or you can simply consider the source, forget about it, and go on about your business. It may be *uncomfortable* when a coworker accuses you of not carrying your load, but it's not *terrible*. You don't *have* to believe what he says. He may think you're a lazy slob, but there's no golden tablet that says you *need* to see things the same way he does.

The ability to handle criticism without "losing it" is a useful skill to add to your repertoire of psychological self-defense tactics. But before going any further, I believe it's helpful to distinguish between two types of criticism: *constructive* ("friendly") and *destructive* ("unfriendly"). The first is meant to be helpful, is normally delivered by someone who cares about you and your feelings, and is usually welcome; the second is hurtful, delivered by someone who doesn't care, and is never welcome. Constructive criticism can be quite valuable: its purpose is to help you learn a thing or two about yourself, grow as a person, or improve your performance in a certain area. Destructive criticism is neither valuable nor helpful: its purpose is to belittle, malign, and control you. When people think of "criticism," they tend to conjure up the negative images and feelings associated with the destructive type.

Dealing effectively with either type of criticism involves knowing what to think, say, and do (Warren & Zgourides, 1991). One of the first things you want to ask yourself when criticized is, "Is this person's criticism valid?" Many times people give each other constructive criticism because they care about and want to help each other. So there's always the possibility that a particular criticism may be true. Then again, people are imperfect and sometimes give each other invalid criticism. Only you can decide what you'll accept as true and what you won't. In the end, regardless of the content of the criticism, it's always important to remember that every person is entitled to his or her own opinion.

Let's take a closer look at how this works. If Linda tells Dave she thinks he's afraid to stand up to his boss and ask for a raise, Dave would ask himself, "Am I afraid of my boss?" If his answer is "Yes," he need not start a fight with Linda, or get down on himself for being a fallible human being. Dave accepts Linda's remarks as constructive feedback and an opportunity for personal growth. If, on the other hand, Dave's answer is "No," he still doesn't have to fly off the handle or berate Linda or himself. Dave remembers that Linda, too, is a fallible human being, and subject to making the same sorts of mistakes as he. Both Dave and Linda may never be able to prove who is right on this particular point, but they can agree to live and let live, accepting that they have differing opinions.

At the heart of oversensitivity to criticism lie numerous *musts* of perfection, approval, and comfort. Learning to tolerate criticism, then, involves rigorously disputing and challenging your Crazy-Makers (CMs) of *demandingness*. The three primary CMs related to criticism are:

1. I *must* be absolutely perfect in every respect, otherwise I'm not a good person, and no one will love me.
2. Others *must* accept and approve of me in every respect, otherwise I'm not a good person, and life isn't worth living.
3. I *must* only hear what I want to hear, as I can't tolerate the discomfort of listening to someone tell me about my faults.

It's also important not to take criticism personally, which is what most people do. Generally, the criticizer is commenting on something that you're doing, not on who you are as an individual. The trouble begins, though, when you *personalize* the criticism (i.e., when you apply what the other person says about your behavior to your worth as a person). If you are ever tempted to do this, keep in mind that *you aren't what other people say or think.* Just because someone says you eat like a hog doesn't mean *you actually are* a hog. So why believe you're a bad or villainous person just because someone else says so? Stick to the facts, and say NO to the rest of it. You'll save yourself a lot of headaches in the long run.

Now that we've seen how to *think* more realistically about criticism, here are some pointers (including sample dialogues) on what to *do* and *say* when you're criticized:

1. Use PARAPHRASING to let the criticizer know that you hear him or her and are interested in what they have to say. It's very easy to respond to criticism by retaliating — returning jabs, attacks, and complaints to the criticizer — which rarely facilitates meaningful dialogue. It's much better to show the other person a little respect.

   Linda: I'm sick and tired of your never picking up after yourself! You're a slob!
   Dave: Oh yeah? You should talk, Ms. Perfect! I'm fed up with your always leaving the toilet seat down. (retaliating)

   versus

   Dave: I get the feeling you're angry at me. You'd like me to pick up more after myself. Am I hearing you correctly? (PARAPHRASING; REALITY CHECKING)
   Linda: Yes.

Dave: Okay, let's talk about it.

Which of Dave's responses do you think will spark a good argument, and which will open up some quality dialogue? That's right — Response #1 starts the fireworks; Response #2 an effective discussion. The beauty of the PARAPHRASING demonstrated in #2 is you don't have to agree with or admit to whatever it is you're being accused of. You simply summarize your accuser's comments; he or she feels heard, you save face, and both of you avoid getting into a fight.

2. If you don't understand why the other person is criticizing you, use DETAILING to get to the bottom of his or her complaints. If after taking an honest look at yourself you conclude that the criticism is valid, then nondefensively *accept* it and *thank* the person for their input! You don't have to rationalize your behavior or make excuses for goofing up. As a fallible human being, it's okay to acknowledge your faults. The idea here is to keep an open mind to the possibility that the feedback may be true, and if so, try to learn what you can from it.

Dave: You're angry at me for being a slob. Exactly how am I a slob? (PARAPHRASING; DETAILING)
Linda: You leave hair in the sink after you shave, and you never pick up your clothes.
Dave: You're right. I do tend to leave a mess in the sink after I shave. And I don't always pick up my clothes. Thanks for letting me know that this stuff bothers you. I'll work on it.
Linda: Thanks for listening.

In this case, Dave is in complete control of his thoughts, feelings, and actions. He empowers himself by freely choosing how he deals with Linda's criticism. He could have reacted by shouting back, leaving home, or threatening divorce (the typical things people do), but he instead chose to keep his cool and avoid a fight by using his psychological self-defense skills.

3. If for some reason you think that the other person's criticism isn't valid, *calmly* point this out. Bear in mind that you can disagree without being disagreeable.

   Dave: You never think about anyone but yourself.
   Linda: I know you're upset right now and feeling a little neglected. And I can accept that, since I've been so busy with these invitations. But in all honesty, I believe I spend a great deal of time meeting other people's needs. What would you like me to do to help you feel better about my schedule?

4. If you find yourself getting agitated and irritated, or about to explode when criticized, you might want to take a quick TIME-OUT (or an extended one, depending on the situation) before getting into it. Time away from an uncomfortable situation allows you to cool your temper (or other strong emotions) while you collect your thoughts. It also gives the other person a chance to calm down and prepare for a meaningful discussion.

   Dave: I have a thing or two to tell you, Linda. You know, you've really been getting on my nerves lately. First off, you're...
   Linda: I need to take a TIME-OUT. Let's talk in a few minutes, okay?
   Dave: Well... sure.

5. Finally, as I mentioned in Chapter 4, effective communication involves two people (a "sender" and a "receiver") engaged in a dynamic interaction in which both parties are on equal terms. Unfortunately, when it comes to criticism, people aren't always so cordial or scientific. A lot of folks like to get things off their chest immediately (which is okay, except when it hurts or invalidates someone else). So they jump at any chance to criticize, even if the other person isn't in the mood to listen to it. If you plan to offer some feedback, try asking first. And if you notice that the other person isn't ready or interested, *don't push it! Unsolicited criticism is a major source of conflict between people!* Chances are you'll get your point across to the other person if you'll wait until the timing is good for both of you.

So much for friendly criticism. Now let's examine some of the techniques that can be used to deal with the type of criticism everybody hates...

COGNITIVE REFRAMING CHART
("Friendly Criticism")

Situation:

Crazy-Maker:
Dispute:
Sensible Reply:

Situation:

Crazy-Maker:
Dispute:
Sensible Reply:

Situation:

Crazy-Maker:
Dispute:
Sensible Reply:

Situation:

Crazy-Maker:
Dispute:
Sensible Reply:

Chapter 15
Learning to Handle
Unfriendly Criticism

Criticism — a big bite out of someone's back.
— Elia Kazan

In the last chapter, I described some simple ways to deal with constructive criticism. But what if the other person doesn't mean well? How do you handle those ugly darts your opponent throws at your self-esteem, self-respect, and personhood? Obviously, your self-defense strategies are going to differ when you're on the receiving end of destructive criticism. As a friend of mine once put it, "Serious times necessitate serious action!"

As I've described in earlier chapters, most Americans hold to the ridiculous premise that you *have* to reply to or answer every comment that comes along. "The System" says answering others is polite. It's a social grace. So if I make a smart remark and put you on the defensive, you *must* reply — not because you want to, but because society says you're *supposed* to. Rationally speaking, where's the law that says you *must* be polite, especially when somebody's taking jabs at you? There isn't any such law, and you can use this to your advantage if you're sick and tired of feeling like a doormat.

In addition to the reframing techniques described in the last chapter, there are advanced assertiveness techniques that can help you take control of destructive criticism. Here are some of my favorites:

1. The first technique involves intentionally ignoring your opponent with SILENCE. For example, you might keep quiet, avoid looking at him or her, and continue on as usual. Or you could use the STARE, in which you say nothing and stare at your opponent when he makes his comment. Remember not to show any emotions (negative or positive) when you use the STARE; simply appear indifferent.

   Further, you might try the ICE-COLD GLARE, in which you say nothing, stare, and sneer at your opponent. More times than not, your friend will soon feel pretty uncomfortable; he's expecting you to say something and probably doesn't like the look on your face. Just keep reminding yourself that there's no demand for you to say anything or look happy.

   The ICE-COLD GLARE works even better when there are innocent bystanders present. Let's say your opponent directs his or her comments at you in front of a bunch of people, and they see you in "icy" action. Guess who appears in control of the situation, and who comes out looking like a fool! Use this technique enough, and the person will probably leave you alone. Mastering SILENCE to cope with criticism takes some practice, but the rewards are well worth the effort. Consider this example of icy SILENCE:

   Karl: (standing over Phil, who is seated at his desk) Phil, you know what, you're worthless! (said jokingly, but meant sarcastically)
   Phil: (remaining silent; ignores Karl and keeps on working) (SILENCE)
   Karl: Didn't you hear me? I said you're worthless!
   Phil: (remaining silent) (SILENCE)
   Karl: (shouting; others in the office look at Karl, who starts feeling embarrassed) I said you're worthless!
   Phil: (still silent) (SILENCE)

Karl: (pauses; now also perspiring) ...Are you okay? Are you mad or something?

Phil: (still silent) (SILENCE)

Karl: Come on, guy, I didn't mean it. You know, I was just joking.

Phil: (says quietly and indifferently, without ever looking up at Karl) I don't have time to chat right now.

At this point, Karl will either stand there and continue to make a fool of himself, or he'll leave. In either case, Phil is the winner.

2. Another very valuable technique for dealing with destructive criticism is the REFLECTING QUESTION, or the "What-Is-It-About...?" counter, also based on the notion that every question deserves an answer. Here, your opponent's remarks are met with a question that reflects what he or she just said. The REFLECTING QUESTION is appropriate when you choose to respond verbally to your opponent's criticisms. Let's see how this one works:

Paula: What an ugly dress you're wearing.

Kathy: What is it about my dress that's ugly? (REFLECTING QUESTION)

Paula: For one thing, the colors clash.

Kathy: What is it about clashing colors that's ugly? (REFLECTING QUESTION)

Paula: They make the dress look cheap.

Kathy: What is it about clashing colors that makes the dress look cheap? (REFLECTING QUESTION)

Paula: Clashing colors make you look like a cheap tramp.

Kathy: What is it about clashing colors that makes me look like a cheap tramp? (REFLECTING QUESTION)

Get the idea? You take whatever your opponent says (exact wording if possible), and you repeat it back to him or her in the form of a question. Your opponent, believing every question must be answered, keeps trying to answer and explain his or her point of view. In other words, you shift the power of the confrontation in your favor; you put your opponent on the defensive, instead of vice-versa. And believe me, there's no way your opponent can win against the RE-FLECTING QUESTION. He or she will back themselves into a corner every time!

With a little practice, the REFLECTING QUESTION can be one of your most valuable self-defense tools. Consider this next example:

Winston: Man, you walk like a fairy.
Lamar: What is it about my walking that makes me look like a fairy? (REFLECTING QUESTION)
Winston: You swish around like a fairy.
Lamar: What is it about my swishing around that makes me look like a fairy? (REFLECTING QUESTION)
Winston: You swing your rear, just like a fairy.
Lamar: What is it about swinging my rear that makes me look like a fairy? (REFLECTING QUESTION)
Winston: (pausing) ...I don't know, man, you just look like a fairy when you walk.
Lamar: What is it about my walking that makes me look like a fairy? (REFLECTING QUESTION)
Winston: Never mind.

Again, there's no way out for the opponent, except to lay off or change the subject.

3. Finally, if you're easily caught off guard by other people's hostile criticisms, you might want to have handy one or more READY REPLIES (RRs). As explained in other chapters, RRs give you a chance to gather your wits and think your way out of an uncomfortable situation. But you have to practice them over and over until they become automatic. That way, you don't have to think to use them. Again, compare this with the martial artist who learns *katas* (i.e., patterns and forms) so that he won't waste valuable time in a dangerous situation trying to decide what to do. The following are a few of my prized RRs for handling unfriendly criticism:

"Hmmm."
"Really?"
"I hear you."

"I don't have time to talk right now."
"Let's talk about it later."
"You sound (or look) upset."
"Bad day?"
"Well, you know how it is."

Having a grasp on how to deal with unfriendly criticism can be a real ego booster. There's great security in knowing that you can handle any and all of those nasty, critical jabs that opponents send your way.

COGNITIVE REFRAMING CHART
("Unfriendly Criticism")

Situation:

Crazy-Maker:
Dispute:
Sensible Reply:

Situation:

Crazy-Maker:
Dispute:
Sensible Reply:

Situation:

Crazy-Maker:
Dispute:
Sensible Reply:

Situation:

Crazy-Maker:
Dispute:
Sensible Reply:

Chapter 16
Refuse to Feel
Needlessly Guilty or Depressed

Do what you can, with what you have, where you are.
— **Theodore Roosevelt**

Guilt. The mere mention of the word brings to mind highly negative images for most people. Painful memories. Feelings of regret and remorse. Self-blame and criticism. Thoughts of sin and failure. The litany goes on and on.

The topic of guilt is particularly dear to my heart, as I'm no stranger to this emotion. In case you haven't noticed from my last name (George *Zgourides,* from the Greek, meaning "kinky hair"!), I'm of Greek-American ancestry. And although I'm proud to have strong ethnic roots, with every pro there comes a con! We've all heard of "Jewish guilt." But have you ever heard of "Greek guilt" or "Greek tragedy"? Well, my friend, Greek guilt is *just as real* as Jewish, Italian, Turkish, or any other type of "Mediterranean" guilt. (There's something about Mediterranean families that promotes guilt — I'm not sure if anyone's ever been able to explain it.) Here are some of the guilt triggers I've been exposed to over the years, courtesy of various well-meaning Guilterizers — relatives, friends, teachers, neighbors, and fellow Churchgoers:

"Shame on you!"
"You always have to do what you're told."
"You must never question the rules."
"You don't make enough money."
"Nice people don't think (or act) like that."

— which, have prompted me (and many, many others) to believe Crazy-Makers (CMs) like:

- If only I hadn't done this or that. I'm a sorry person and a shame to everyone around me.
- If only I did what I'm told. I don't, so I'm nothing more than a rebellious ingrate.
- I shouldn't question the rules. I do, so I'm a worthless person who wants to upset the establishment.
- If only I made more money. As is, I don't, so I'm a failure.
- If only I thought (or acted) like a nice person. I don't always, so that means I'm a bad person.

Of course, these kinds of CMs aren't the exclusive domain of Greek-Americans. You find them among people of all races, creeds, and backgrounds. I use my fellow ethnics as an example, because I've lived the Greek scene. However, I'm confident you too can relate to at least a few of the above, and probably come up with some of your own.

From my discussion thus far, it might sound like I believe all guilt is bad. Not at all! Like so many emotions, guilt has both positive and negative sides; specifically, *constructive* ("rational") and *destructive* ("irrational") guilt. Constructive guilt is present-focused and results from an intact conscience, which tells you right from wrong and pushes you to correct your wrongdoings. With so many sociopaths loose on the streets, I believe our society could really use more constructive guilt.

Destructive guilt, on the other hand, is past-focused and results from an overactive conscience, which tells you everything you do is wrong and pushes you to overcorrect for your wrongdoings (or at least try to). It keeps you stuck in the past so that you can't make effective decisions in the present. You become so focused on trying to make-up for yesterday's mistakes that you are blinded to today's happenings.

Self-talk like, "I've been so bad that I can never do enough to make-up for things!" is typical of destructive guilt, the main subject of this chapter.

So where does destructive guilt come from? What's behind this negative emotion? And what are some of the consequences of feeling guilty? Essentially, guilt is just another expression of irrational, absolutistic thinking. Unlike anxiety's *what ifs* (future-focus), guilt has as its core beliefs various *if onlys* (past-focus). For instance:

- If only I had lived up to my potential!
- If only I had treated my mother better while she was alive!
- If only I were smarter!

— which translate into:

- I *should* have lived up to my potential.
- I *should* have treated my mother better while she was alive.
- I *should* have worked harder in school so I'd be smarter.

— which all imply:

- My past *must* determine how I think and what I do in present, and continue to do so forever.
- I *must* find the perfect solution to yesterday's problems.
- I'm a rotten, worthless person for failing to do or be what I *should* do or be, or *should* have done or been.

We see from these sample CMs that irrational guilt begins with arbitrary *shoulds* and *musts,* and ends with self-loathing and blaming. Why? Because irrational guilt is a strong motivator, but it's the wrong motivator. Instead of promoting personal growth, it pushes people into trying to live up to someone else's standards. And, of course, we know what happens when you try to do that! You *fail!* And when you fail, you feel like a *failure*! And when you feel like a failure, you become *depressed*! And when you become depressed, you *self-blame* and *self-berate*! And when you blame yourself and berate yourself, you feel *guilty* for being imperfect and fallible! In other words, a guilt reaction is a vicious, self-defeating cycle that fuels itself each time you give in to irrational thinking, saying, and doing.

Can anything be done about guilt and its cousin, depression? Certainly! If everyone lived according to Theodore Roosevelt's "Do-What-You-Can-With-What-You-Have-Where-You-Are"   principle, there'd be much less needless guilt and depression in our world. Why? Because of one simple idea — *acceptance*. While working to improve our lives and society, we'd *accept* our imperfections and limitations. We'd *accept* that we're going to make mistakes. We'd *accept* that others aren't always going to treat us fairly. We'd *accept* that life isn't always going to give us what we want, when we want it. Embracing acceptance in this way eliminates guilt and depression, and leads to a rewarding, productive, and assertive life.

I offer you a few of Dr. Z.'s pointers for dealing with and overcoming these two destructive emotions:

1. Decide that needless guilt and depression are just that — *needless!* See them as negative influences that are best eliminated from your life.
2. Be realistic in your appraisals of the past. The best move is to *accept* the fact that *you did what you could, with what you had, where you were.* It's very easy to look back and negatively reevaluate what happened in the past. And when you let people push your guilt buttons, it's even easier to blow the negative aspects of an event way out of proportion (called *magnification,* described in Chapter 2). Remember the saying, "Hindsight is always 20-20."
3. Employ cognitive reframing to change your assumptions about 1) your past *having* to determine your present and future; 2) your *needing* to find a perfect solution to yesterday's problems; and 3) your *requiring* yourself to feel like an incompetent and a failure. In other words, cast out your devilish *if onlys, shoulds,* and *musts!*
4. Have the courage to stand up to your Guilterizers, whether it's a boss, Sunday school teacher, or your sweet and innocent grandmother. It's okay to be polite, but don't back down! When someone tries to control or manipulate you with guilt, graciously refuse the invitation! Then meet their commands with any of a number of Self-Defense Responses, such as PROCESS COMMENTS, READY REPLIES, or deliberate SILENCE. For example:

Student: You just have to give me a better grade; otherwise, my GPA will miss the cut-off, and I'll lose my scholarship. You're the only one who'll listen and can help me.
Professor: I get the sense you're trying to push my sympathy buttons to talk me into giving you a grade you didn't earn. (PROCESS COMMENT)

and

Mother: Wouldn't you rather cancel your trip to Mexico next week and stay home and clean closets with me? Remember, I've always been there for you.
Daughter: Oh, well, you know how it is. (READY REPLY)

and

Father: You never could do anything right as a child. You're a complete failure.
Son: (saying nothing and looking away) (SILENCE)

5. Have the courage to admit that you're a fallible human being and *forgive yourself* for your sins, wrongdoings, mistakes, imperfections, faults, shortcomings, inadequacies, and deficiencies. As I've pointed out many times before, accepting your fallible nature is vital to achieving mental and emotional freedom.

6. Finally, and perhaps most importantly, *practice* the above techniques until they become second nature to you.

COGNITIVE REFRAMING CHART
("Guilt and Depression")

Situation:

Crazy-Maker:
Dispute:
Sensible Reply:

Situation:

Crazy-Maker:
Dispute:
Sensible Reply:

Situation:

Crazy-Maker:
Dispute:
Sensible Reply:

Situation:

Crazy-Maker:
Dispute:
Sensible Reply:

Part III
When Others Psych You Out

Chapter 17

At Home

If you cannot get rid of the family skeleton,
you may as well make it dance.
— **George Bernard Shaw**

Whenever people are involved with one another — be it living, socializing, or working together — they are in a *relationship*. And where there is a relationship, there is the potential for interpersonal conflicts. Spouses, children, immediate family, step-families, distant relatives, friends, neighbors, bosses, supervisors, employees, coworkers, teachers, and students — no one is immune. Ironically, one of society's most popular myths is that being in any type of relationship means you *should* always get along, that you *should* never disagree or argue.

Nowhere are relationship conflicts more evident than at home. Let's face it, when it comes to family — and it doesn't matter if it's your spouse, your Aunt Tilly, or your ex-wife's cousin-in-law twice removed — disagreements (some of which are bound to turn into arguments) are going to arise. Yet this isn't necessarily all bad news. Although usually unpleasant at the time, arguments and quarrels *of the occasional sort* can help a relationship grow and mature. However, most family members and couples don't engage in such *constructive* arguing. They instead use their conflicts to belittle, accuse, whine, and insult each other. Such vicious, *destructive* arguing is useless and unproductive, often leading to long-term unhappiness and dissatisfaction within a relationship.

Using the psychological self-defense strategies outlined in ***Don't Let Them Psych You Out!*** can help you avert destructive conflicts, or at least resolve them with minimal harm done to the relationship. For example, couples who practice effective communication experience increased intimacy and understanding, as well as relational growth. Why? Because they communicate their needs and wants in an honest, caring, and rational manner. It is the judicious person, then, who uses psychological self-defense to meet what can be one of the most challenging aspects of any relationship — those inevitable interpersonal conflicts.

Let's take a look at some methods for dealing with disagreements and improving your family relationships:

1. Decide to make your family relationships the best they can be. You'll never have a 100% perfect, trouble-free home life, but you can work to improve what's there by applying your cognitive self-defense skills. As Dale Carnegie once said, "Happiness doesn't depend upon who you are or what you have, it depends solely upon what you think."

2. Remember that every relationship is different. Therefore, be familiar with the personalities of various difficult family members whom you are likely to encounter at home (i.e., your "family opponents"), and then deal with them accordingly. Although there are many variations of family opponents, here are four jewels:

    a. *The Guilterizer relative.* The Guilterizer family member tries to achieve his or her ends by pushing your guilt buttons. He or she tries to play on your sympathy and pity, generally hitting on you in moments of weakness, when your defenses are down. A common example of the Guilterizer in action is the relative who tells you he needs to borrow money to pay his rent or he'll be evicted. Then when you loan him the money, he blows it on a new stereo instead.

b. *The Complainer relative.* This one is continually griping about something, from not having enough money to the government being corrupt. The Complainer comes across as a person with a very negative attitude about life. Spending time with a Complainer is usually a drag, explaining why other family members run in the opposite direction when they see him or her coming.

c. *The Criticizer relative.* This one loves to find fault with who you are and everything you're doing. Nothing about you is right. The Criticizer is similar to the Complainer, except that the caustic remarks are directed at you personally.

d. *The Savior relative.* The Savior family member plays the role of the martyr. He or she is always making personal sacrifices to rescue others, even if they don't want any help. And if you throw a Hysteric into the Savior's family system, you end up with an "I'll-Rescue-You-Whenever-You-Stir-Up-Chaos" family script. Savior relatives are sometimes called "codependents."

3. Use cognitive reframing to challenge your irrationalities about getting along with family. The three most common "At Home" Crazy-Makers (CMs) are:

- I *must* get along with all of my loved ones under all circumstances. If I don't, I'm a *terrible* person, and *life isn't worth living.*
- My family *must* think, talk, and act they way I want them to. If they don't, they're *rotten* and *deserve severe punishment.*
- My home life *must* give me what I desire, easily and without effort or frustration. If it doesn't, it's *awful*, and *I won't be able to stand it.*

Recognize these CMs? Yes, they are variations of Albert Ellis' "musturbatory ideology":

- *I must have what I want, when I want, and on my terms only!*
- *Others must do what I want, when I want, and on my terms only!*
- *Life must give me what I want, when I want, and on my terms only!*

And what do these *musts* lead to? Besides mental and emotional misery, they lead to *awfulizing, catastrophizing, disasterizing,* and *terriblelizing,* followed by *I-Can't-Take-It-Another-Minuteitis,* or *low frustration tolerance.* The pattern goes something like this:

- I *must...*
- If I don't, then it's *awful...*
- And if it's awful, then I *won't be able to stand it.*

What a pile of nonsense! Fortunately, you can use your cognitive reframing techniques to break this kind of crazy pattern. For instance:

- Who says I *must...?*
- And if I don't, where's the proof that it'll be *awful...?*
- And even if it were awful, where's the law that says *I won't be able to stand it...?*

And the answers to these questions are:

- *Nobody!*
- *There isn't any proof!!*
- *There isn't any such law!!!*

4. Use Self-Defense Responses to respond to difficult family members. It's usually best to start with less intimidating ones. Here's an example of how to use NICE NOs, the TAPE LOOP, and LIMIT-SETTING with a Guilterizer relative who asks to borrow money:

Nephew Ron: Uncle John, I really need $250 by next week, or the lien holder is going to repossess my car. Please help me. You're the only one I can turn to!

Uncle John: What happened to the money I gave you two weeks ago?

Nephew Ron: Well, I had to spend it on some other things.

Uncle John: I'd like to help you again, but I can't. (NICE NO)

Nephew Ron: But please! My dad says you're loaded.

Uncle John: Like I said, I'd like to help you, but I can't. (TAPE LOOP)

Nephew Ron: But I'm desperate. I've gotta have a car to get to work.

Uncle John: Ron, you could always take the bus.

Nephew Ron: Maybe to work, but I've also got a big date next week.

Uncle John: Because you're so desperate, why don't you try borrowing money from your bank?

Nephew Ron: I tried. They wouldn't loan me any money because of my bad credit.

Uncle John: If your bank, which is in the business of loaning money, thinks you're a bad credit risk, how could I possibly loan you money? I'm not in the banking business. I'd like to help, but it's just not a good idea. Sorry. (LIMIT-SETTING; NICE NO)

Nephew Ron: But we're family!

Uncle John: Family or not, I'm not a banker. And I still think it's a bad idea. (TAPE LOOP)

Nephew Ron: But you've just gotta help me out, just this once!

Uncle John: Tell you what I'll do. If you'll take the bus to work, I'll be happy to give you a lift on your date next week.

Nephew Ron: Never mind, Uncle John.

Although Uncle John sounds cold and callous in this example, he chooses to stand his ground and not loan his nephew any more money. Unfortunately, although his nephew may have every intention of paying his uncle back, if Ron's like 90% of the people in our society who "borrow" money from family, Uncle John might as well kiss goodbye any hard-earned dollars he loans to Ron.

5. A good number of relationship conflicts occur between romantic partners (both married and live-in couples). To minimize the possibility of conflicts arising...

First, know what it is about romantic relationships that helps them last. According to Nathaniel Branden (1988, pp. 225-228) and other experts, couples who stay in love for long periods of time share the following characteristics:

a. They express their love verbally.
b. They express their love sexually.
c. They express their love materially (e.g., with gifts; sharing chores).
d. They are physically affectionate.
e. They express their admiration and affection.
f. They are mutually self-disclosing.
g. They accept one another's shortcomings and demands.
h. They offer one another emotional support.
i. They make time to be alone together.

Second, consider the following recommendations for resolving your relationship conflicts:

a. As a couple, identify the problems in your relationship and agree to work them out together by practicing effective communication (Chapter 4).
b. Take active responsibility for finding a solution to your problems. Avoiding issues and conflicts only makes things worse in the long run.

c. Re-evaluate your expectations for the relationship. Expecting too much or too little from your partner or yourself can be a major source of conflict for both parties.

d. Determine what it is you want out of the relationship, but also respect your partner's freedom to determine what he or she wants out of the relationship.

e. Practice tolerance. Nobody's perfect, so why get upset when you or your partner make mistakes? Remember the two rules of life — *Rule #1*: Don't sweat the small stuff; *Rule #2*: It's all small stuff!

f. Remind yourself that, although it's easier to focus on the negative things people do, it's more helpful to build on the positive. In other words, keep a realistic perspective about it all.

g. Don't get into the "Blaming" game. Accept responsibility for your own actions, and try giving your partner the benefit of the doubt.

h. Don't give in to the idea that working through problems is "easier said than done." After generating alternatives and deciding on a solution, see it through! This is frequently the hardest part for couples to do.

i. Don't hesitate to seek the services of a professional therapist to help you overcome relationship obstacles. (See Appendix B for tips on how to find a reputable mental health therapist.)

j. Hang in there as long as both of you think there's a possibility of the relationship working. However, there's no point to staying with a sinking ship. There may come a time when you both should go your separate ways.

6. Besides money, one of the most popular topics of disagreement for couples is *sex* — specifically, issues of *how often*, *what time*, *where*, and *which activity*. And one of the negative side effects of sexual (and general relationship) disagreements is one or both partners developing a sexual problem (e.g., impotence in men; inability to orgasm in women). Fortunately,

sexual problems are preventable and treatable! Consider the following recommendations for preventing and overcoming this kind of problem:

a. Keep the lines of communication open between you and your partner. Practice expressing your feelings, preferences, likes, and dislikes to one another.

b. Challenge your personal irrational attitudes and beliefs about sexuality. Remember that your sexual values and preferences come from a variety of sources, many of them dating back to early childhood. Knowing where you're coming from can help you figure out where you're going.

c. Avoid setting sexual performance goals. Don't make unrealistic performance demands of yourself, such as *having* to engage in rigorous coitus every night. And don't fall into the trap of making orgasm (the "Big O") the all-important goal of sex.

d. Avoid *spectatoring* (i.e., monitoring your sexual actions by "stepping outside" of your body and watching yourself). Instead, enjoy the erotic sensations of lovemaking, in whatever form. Keep in mind that there's no right or wrong way to have sex — it's up to you and your partner to decide what you both find appealing and comfortable.

e. Avoid comparing yourself to others or sex statistics. "Locker-room" talk is usually just that — *talk!*

f. Take time out for sex. There's no need to rush (unless you and your partner want to). Relax and enjoy!

g. Never hesitate to seek out professional help for a sexual problem. And usually the earlier this is done, the better. A false sense of modesty or embarrassment about sexual matters is no reason to suffer in silence. Keep in mind the saying, "In our secrets lie our sickness." Don't be afraid to talk things out, both with your partner and a professional therapist. (See Appendix C for tips on how to find a reputable sex therapist.)

COGNITIVE REFRAMING CHART
("At Home")

Situation:

Crazy-Maker:
Dispute:
Sensible Reply:

Situation:

Crazy-Maker:
Dispute:
Sensible Reply:

Situation:

Crazy-Maker:
Dispute:
Sensible Reply:

Situation:

Crazy-Maker:
Dispute:
Sensible Reply:

Chapter 18

Near Home

Love thy neighbor as thyself,
but choose your neighborhood.

— Louise Beal

Friends and neighbors can be great. Parties. Afternoon get-togethers. Barbecues. Softball. Phone chats. A shared cup of coffee in the morning. There's something about socializing that increases the quality of life. Personally, I love nothing better than a fun evening out on the town with one or more of my pals.

But as you're well aware, the social picture isn't always a pretty one. Like everything else in life, there's a downside to friends and neighbors. Pure and simple, it's human nature for people to get on each others' nerves, although this seems especially true of those who are involved at some level — be it in a familial, social, or working relationship.

If you've ever had a friend pester you for money, or a neighbor encourage his dog to poop in your flower bed, then you know that social relationships can be trying — *very trying*. They can even seem *impossible* at times. I know this story all too well. There have been times in my life when various relationships have been so trying —

well-intentioned friends and acquaintances pulling at me from every direction — that I've seriously considered throwing everything I own into my truck and moving to the desert to become a hermit. And I realize I'm not the only one who feels this way. We've all had to deal with imposing friends and noisy neighbors. The good news, however, is that with patience and careful use of the self-defense techniques described throughout this book, you can learn to take charge of your social relationships.

Even if you have basically good, solid social relationships, you're still going to have problems. Here's a Dr. Z. example to illustrate this point. I tend to be a fairly sociable guy. In addition to spending time with friends and family, I enjoy meeting new and interesting people. So I'm constantly attending this or that function, and striking up conversations with people I don't know. Unfortunately, it has taken me a long time to realize that just because *some* socializing is good, *more* socializing isn't necessarily *better*. And have I learned this one the hard way! Let me explain.

When I first moved to Oregon several years ago to complete my doctoral psychology training, I found myself alone and lonely. Far away from home. Not knowing a soul within 1,500 miles in any direction. Living in a dreadfully depressing single room apartment with no windows or shower (all I could afford at the time) in Forest Grove, Oregon.

After a few months of not knowing anyone (other than casual acquaintances from my classes), I decided it was time to take action to improve my situation. I went on a "Shake-Hands-Meet-People-Get-Involved" campaign at my campus and church. I introduced myself to everyone I could. I joined two bands and a university chorus. I premiered a small orchestra piece and did a little conducting with a local ensemble. I attended aerobics class. I went to "happy hours" on Friday nights. I sang in the Greek choir on Sundays. I showed up at every party, musical event, and get-together I could. *My plan worked!* Within one year, I had more friends than I knew what to do with. My social life in Oregon had suddenly gone from waiting all week to say "Hi" to the check-out person at the grocery store to double-booking myself with friends evenings and weekends, seven days a week.

Sounds like a social butterfly's dream-come-true, doesn't it? In many ways my years in doctoral school were the best ever. (However, I don't want to leave you with the impression that I did nothing but socialize in graduate school. During this time, I also managed to get my doctoral studies done, see clients, and publish several professional articles.) Then something happened I never expected; I began experiencing what scientists term the *entropy effect*, which refers to the tendency for events in life to go from a state of order to one of total disorder. And "entropy" pretty much sums up my social life the last few years. Even these days, it isn't unusual for me to come home after a long, grueling day of teaching or seeing clients, only to find a dozen phone messages from friends calling to see how I'm doing or wanting to get together. People mean well, and I love and appreciate them, but it still doesn't make returning a dozen calls and declining invitations any easier. But, of course, that's where psychological self-defense can help.

In my case, and probably yours too, I usually prefer not to hurt my friends' feelings by ignoring their invites, telling them to leave me alone, or using intimidating self-defense techniques (e.g., the ICE-COLD GLARE) on them. I wouldn't appreciate a friend doing that to me. Instead, I choose to be assertive, but in a delicate, nonaggressive way. Dealing with people you care about — friends, family, or whomever — can at times seem like a fine balancing act.

Although the majority of suggestions from the last chapter, "At Home," also apply to friends and neighbors, here are a few additional particulars for assertively handling those you'll find "Near Home":

1. As with family, accept that disagreements will arise, even among the best of friends. Remember, it's normal and healthy to disagree. You can even do so without being disagreeable!

2. Recognize typical personalities and tactics of "Near Home" opponents. Maybe you know or live next to one or more of these characters:

   a. *The Exploiter friend.* The Exploiter friend is the one who's always imposing, asking you for slightly excessive favors — not enough to ruin your friendship, but just enough to take advantage of it. The typical Exploiter is an expert at reading his friends, deciding which are the "nice" ones, and then talking them into giving, loaning, or going "above and beyond" the usual. The scary part is that he has the ability to make his "requests" sound perfectly reasonable.

b. *The Value-Pusher friend.* This friend insists that you share his values, morals, ethics, and general life interests. If he takes up a politically incorrect cause, then so should you. If he plays water polo for hours on end, then so should you. If he believes in the tooth fairy, then so should you. You still like your Value-Pusher friend, but you're careful not to bring up controversial topics when you're together.

c. *The Button-Pusher neighbor.* The Button-Pusher neighbor does whatever he can to get under your skin. Why? To show you who's in charge of the neighborhood. How? By identifying and turning your weak spots against you. An example of a Button-Pusher in action is the neighbor who one night, just for the heck of it, "accidentally" drives over and crushes your new garbage cans as they sit in the street for the next morning's pickup.

d. *The Passive-Aggressor neighbor.* This guy tells you one thing, but thinks and does the exact opposite. Why? To get you off his back by telling you what you want to hear. The neighbor who promises you he'll move the rusted-out motorhome from his front yard, but has no intention of ever doing so, falls into this category.

3. Challenge your "Near Home" Crazy-Makers (CMs):

- I *must* get along with all of my friends and neighbors under all circumstances. If I don't, I'm a *terrible* person, and *life isn't worth living.*
- My friends and neighbors *must* think and act the way I want them to. If they don't, they're *rotten* and *deserve severe punishment.*
- My social life *must* give me what I desire, easily and without effort or frustration. If it doesn't, it's *awful,* and *I won't be able to stand it.*

Notice that these CMs are virtually identical to the "At Home" ones we identified in the last chapter. And remember where we said most CMs come from? That's right, from those irrational assumptions of *demandingness* you and I have about self, others, and life:

- *I must have what I want, when I want, and on my terms only!*
- *Others must do what I want, when I want, and on my terms only!*
- *Life must give me what I want, when I want, and on my terms only!*

Albert Ellis' "musturbatory ideology" strikes again! Regrettably, *musturbating* prompts *awfulizing* and *I-Can't-Take-It-Another-Minuteitis*. Again, here's that nonsensical line of reasoning humans are so fond of:

- I *must...*
- If I don't, then it's *awful...*
- And if it's awful, then *I won't be able to stand it.*

And the rational Disputes to this nonsense:

- Who says I *must...*?
- And if I don't, where's the proof that it'll be *awful...*?
- And even if it were awful, where's the law that says *I won't be able to stand it...*?

And again, the answers to these questions are:

- *Nobody!*
- *There isn't any proof!!*
- *There isn't any such law!!!*

4. As with family, first choose less intimidating self-defense techniques for use with friends and neighbors, only moving to more intimidating ones if necessary. For example, use READY REPLIES (RRs) and NICE NOs to turn down social invitations:

Jill: Dill and I are having a big party next Friday, and we'd like you to drop by.

Phil: I'm really busy these days. Thanks anyway. (READY REPLY)

or

Phil: You know my schedule. I'll have to see how things are going by next Friday. (RR)

or

Phil: I doubt I'll be able to make it over. Thanks anyway. (NICE NO)

or

Phil: I can't make it that night. Maybe some other time. (NICE NO)

Or use RRs to answer personal questions:

Aunt Anita: When on earth are you going to get married? People are beginning to talk.
Niece Norma: Hmmm. (walking off) (RR)

or

Niece Norma: Oh well, you know how it is. (RR)

or

Niece Norma: I really couldn't care less. (RR)

or

Niece Norma: I don't have time to talk right now. (RR)

or

Niece Norma: It's nobody's business. (RR)

5. For dealing with neighbors who aren't your friends, all of the self-defense counters in *Don't Let Them Psych You Out!* — even the intimidating ones — are fair game. For example, use LIMIT-SETTING, INTERRUPTING, or the SMART ALECK with nosy neighbors:

Ding: I saw the appliance store people move a new washer into your house yesterday. How much did it cost?

Ling: I never tell anyone how much I spend on my major purchases. (LIMIT-SETTING)

or

Ling: How much did you say *your* washer cost? (INTER-RUPTING)

or

Ling: Oh, you just reminded me of something I've been wanting to ask you. Could you give me your recipe for sweet-and-sour tuna? (INTERRUPTING)

or

Ling: More than you could ever afford. (SMART ALECK)

6. Noisy neighbors who refuse to quiet down can be an extreme source of irritation. Being forced to listen to someone else's noise pollution, especially when you're trying to read or sleep, is nothing short of mental torture. This was my situation exactly while I was living in that dreadful Forest Grove apartment I described earlier. My place was separated from "Karen's" by a thin piece of plaster, so the amount of noise transfer across apartments was ridiculous. To make matters worse, Karen would come in drunk at all hours of the night, bumping into things and singing off-pitch with the radio at the top of her lungs. Man, was I miserable! I tried confronting her, negotiating, banging on the wall, complaining to the managers (who lived elsewhere), and filing a complaint with the police — but nothing worked. Finally, I moved. Which brings me to my next point...

7. If you believe you're being unduly imposed on by unscrupulous neighbors — whatever the problem — don't just lie there like a piece of lox! Take action, and feel okay about it! Complain to the managers (if applicable) or the neighborhood association, call the police, see an attorney about filing a lawsuit, or even move if you have to (and can). But do something!

Sounds simple enough, but why don't people take action against neighbor opponents? Because of those "Near Home" CMs above, specifically, that "I *must* get along with everybody" and "If I don't, I'm a *failure*." To be sure, complaining or filing charges isn't going to help you get along with obnoxious, inconsiderate neighbors. But think about it. Which alternative is the most likely to get you some peace and quiet at 2:00 a.m. when your neighbors are sponsoring a margarita festival — sitting there with your ear muffs on being irrational, or calling the police?

8. Finally, if for whatever reason nothing works and you can't move, you have a perfect opportunity to work on increasing your frustration tolerance. For example, you could keep reminding yourself that...

• Although irritating, having undesirable neighbors is *inconvenient*, but not *terrible*.
• I'd *prefer* that my neighbors do like I ask, but I don't *demand* it.
• I'm not a *failure* because my neighbors won't do like I ask.

The beauty of psychological self-defense is that, even during those "impossible" situations (and there are a lot of them out there), you can still find answers inside your head.

Cognitive Reframing Chart
("Near Home")

Situation:

Crazy-Maker:
Dispute:
Sensible Reply:

Situation:

Crazy-Maker:
Dispute:
Sensible Reply:

Situation:

Crazy-Maker:
Dispute:
Sensible Reply:

Situation:

Crazy-Maker:
Dispute:
Sensible Reply:

Chapter 19
At Work
and School

Power corrupts the few,
while weakness corrupts the many.

— Eric Hoffer

"My boss is an imbecilic tyrant!"

"If I weren't a religious person, I think I might have killed my CEO by now."

"I just loved it last month when our district manager called to tell us that the home office had decided to cut our secretarial help. He said we're stockbrokers in a small town, and could just do the secretarial work ourselves. What nerve!"

"I literally shake in my boots before I go into work, just knowing my supervisor is going to ride my backside all day. Nothing I ever do is good enough for her."

"I really hate the idea of some supervisor nitpicking to death everything I do, just because he hates women."

"Mr. Ph.D. thinks he's so smart. And he expects his students to focus on his class only, just because he likes the topic. His teaching is frightful, but don't dare question his methods. I tried that early in the semester, and the egotistical jerk has had it in for me ever since."

Like home life, work and school provide fertile soil for interpersonal conflicts. But unlike family and friends with whom we're on a somewhat equal standing, our relationships at work and school are usually lopsided. One person holds a great deal of power, while the other person doesn't. And guess who's generally at the mercy of the other!

Now I'm not saying that conflicts don't arise between employees or students. They do! But more often than not, the misery people experience in their work and school relationships is due to *imbalances of power* and subsequent *conflicts with authority figures.* These may take the form of conflicts between boss and employee, supervisor and supervisee, or teacher and student.

In Chapter 1, I talked about two basic personalities — *drivers,* who tend to control others at all costs, and *amiables,* who tend to please others at all costs. I also noted that bosses, supervisors, teachers, etc. are usually drivers, while the "nice" people under their authority are usually amiables. Of course, these are generalizations, but I do believe this model helps explain why there are so many conflicts in work and school environments. More often than not, the driver pushes the amiable until he explodes back at the driver, who then pushes harder to regain control. And the cycle continues repeating until life becomes so miserable that someone backs down, which in most cases is the amiable — if he wants to keep his job or stay in school.

So why be concerned about this third brand of relationship? Because most of us attend school or work for a living. First, if you attend class, study, or work 40 hours a week, and sleep 8 hours a night, you're spending roughly $1/3$ of your waking hours at school or on the job. And if you're miserable, that adds up to a very significant portion of your time. This is one reason why authority conflicts are such a strain on your psyche — it's hard to get away from them! Second, inherent in any power imbalance is a feeling of helplessness on the part of the person being managed, supervised, or taught. And nobody likes to feel out of control or at the absolute mercy of someone else, especially an individual who not only holds the keys to your academic and financial future, but also knows it!

As we've noted throughout *Don't Let Them Psych You Out!*, you have many strategies available to deal with difficult or "impossible" situations, including mental reframing and an almost infinite number of verbal comebacks. You should keep in mind, though, that authoritarian situations differ somewhat from nonauthoritarian ones. Unlike the person with the power, the one without the power is almost always on the defensive. It's simply the nature of the beast, which doesn't bother the power-holder in the slightest. He or she knows they have you right where they want you, that you have to do what you're told, to avoid being fired or expelled.

The same psychological self-defense principles basically apply in both types of situations; you just have to be slightly more cautious and concerned about the potential ramifications of your actions when confronting an authority figure. For instance, you have much more at stake during a conflict with your boss than with a telephone solicitor. So to be effective (not to mention keep your job), you might choose to steer clear of certain self-defense tactics that, while useful on the phone, might not work to your advantage on the job.

The following are some practical pointers I've found helpful over the years for assertively dealing with "At Work and School" opponents:

1. Accept authoritarian situations for what they are — lopsided power plays. If you can manage to see the situation in a different light, you'll be less stressed about encounters with authority figures.

2. Certainly you've worked for or studied with at least one of the following opponents. There are lots of others, but these four are some of the worst:

   a. *The Power-Monger boss.* The Power-Monger, or Tyrant boss is dominating and overcontrolling. Besides generating misery for everyone in the office, he feels compelled to run his employees' personal lives — from telling them who they may eat lunch with to what they should do in their spare time (if he lets them have any). Also, forget about any compromises with this boss. It's his way, or else!

b. *The Penny-Pincher manager.* This is the manager who expects you to do more and more work with less and less support. For example, you're supposed to increase productivity 20% this year, with 20% less resources than you had last year. The Penny-Pincher usually doesn't mind spending money on himself or his fat cat friends, just so long as he cuts *somewhere,* which usually means your department. Of course, he rationalizes cushioning at the top (e.g., remodeling administrative offices) by convincing himself that he's saving enormous amounts cutting at the bottom (e.g., denying your request for a much-needed second phone line).

c. *The Anal-Retentive supervisor.* The Anal-Retentive supervisor is obsessed with order and cleanliness. This perfectionistic type is a "detail freak" — every "i" must be dotted, and every "t" crossed. Files must be works of art. Reports must be on par with classic literature. Offices must be as clean and orderly as a museum. Because perfection is the norm, any employee who doesn't give 120% is subject to extra supervisory "attention," frequently in the form of criticism and belittling. Unfortunately, the more the employee resists, the more he or she is beat up emotionally. Related to the Anal-Retentive supervisor is the Hawk supervisor, who monitors everything everybody does for fear that someone might try to "pull a fast one."

d. *The Egotist professor.* The Egotist professor is the one who lectures hours on end without a break, refuses to entertain students' questions, gives excessive homework assignments, is never available outside of class for advising, and frequently breaks appointments with students. Why? Because 1) he assumes his students are just as interested in his boring "ivory tower" topic as he, and 2) he thinks he's so important that there's no need bothering to help his students. Having had 10 years of schooling and being a professor myself, I can tell you first hand that egotism is a significant problem in today's institutions of higher learning.

3. In authoritarian situations, it usually isn't to your advantage to blow up at your boss or professor. First, you can't make good decisions when you're hot under the collar. Second, your opponent has any of a number of weapons he can use against you (like firing you), which he's more likely to do if he thinks you have a bad

attitude or are carrying a grudge. There's a much better way to deal with "At Work and School" opponents — the psychological self-defense way!

First, challenge your Crazy-Makers (CMs) about having to like and get along with your boss or professor, the need to please others, and the terribleness of losing your job, etc. For example:

- I *must* get along with my superiors at work and school.
- I *must* always please my superiors at work and school.
- I *must* keep my job or stay in school, no matter the costs to me and my family.

As usual, demanding *musts* lead to *catastrophizing:*

- If I don't like or get along with my superiors, it'd be *horrible.*
- If I don't always please my superiors, *life isn't worth living.*
- If I lose my job or drop out of school, then I'm a *failure* and an *awful* person.

And to feelings of *low frustration tolerance:*

- If things are horrible, life isn't worth living, and I'm a failure and an awful person, and *I won't be able to stand it.*

We've seen this "Musturbation — Catastrophization — Low Frustration Tolerance" pattern before. The answer to it? Like always, coming up with Disputes for your irrational CMs. For example:

- So what if I don't like or get along with my superiors? What's so *horrible* about that?
- Why do I always need to please my superiors? If for some reason I don't, why does that mean *life isn't worth living?*
- Where's the rule that says if I lose my job or drop out of school that I'm a *failure* and an *awful* person?

And then some Sensible Replies to your Disputes:

- It's *inconvenient* if I don't like or get along with my superiors, but it isn't horrible.
- It may be *uncomfortable* when I don't always please my superiors, but that doesn't mean life isn't worth living.

• It'd be *unfortunate* if I lost my job or dropped out of school, but there isn't any rule that says I'm a failure or awful person because of this.

With respect to this last Dispute and Sensible Reply, some people might take issue with my reframing a job loss as merely *unfortunate* rather than terribly *awful.* Here's an excerpt from a session I recently had with a client who was worried about losing his job:

Carl: Dr. Z., I have bills and mortgage payments due, nothing in savings, and my wife can't work because she has to stay home with our 14-month-old triplets. If I lost my job, we'd be in the poor house within a month. How can losing my job under those circumstances be anything other than disastrous?

Dr. Z.: Sounds like you can't afford to lose your job right now.

Carl: Exactly!

Dr. Z.: Okay, then let's consider what you could do if for some reason you were unexpectedly fired.

Carl: I guess I could start looking for a new job. But you know the teaching market is really tight at the moment. I might not be able to find anything.

Dr. Z.: That's always a possibility. What other jobs could you find?

Carl: I could always go back into sales.

Dr. Z.: And if you couldn't find anything in sales, what else could you do?

Carl: If worse came to worst, I suppose I could work at a fast-food restaurant, but the salaries are too low to support a family.

Dr. Z.: So what could you do to lower your expenses?

Carl: I guess we could move into a cheaper place, sell our new car... you know, cut our monthly expenses.

Dr. Z.: Now you're talking. Where else could you get money?

Carl: Maybe I could look into government assistance, but I'd hate to do that.

Dr. Z.: Sure, but that's what it's there for. Perhaps you could draw unemployment until you found another job.

Carl: I guess.

Dr. Z.: Why, then, is the possibility of losing your job so *disastrous?* It sounds mighty *inconvenient* to me, but hardly life-threatening. You really have a lot of options, don't you?

Carl: Yeah.

Dr. Z.: Anyway, what's the probability that things would get so bad that you lost your job, had to move into a cheaper place, had to sell your car, had to draw unemployment, and then finally had to work at a low-pay fast-food restaurant?

Carl: I guess pretty small. Actually, I'm doing quite well at work. I just hate my boss.

Dr. Z.: So you're worrying about something that probably won't happen.

Carl: Yeah.

Dr. Z.: Well, let's see if we can work on reframing your perceptions so that you don't allow your boss to get under your skin so much.

Carl: Okay.

From this example we see that a seemingly devastating scenario isn't necessarily so when the facts are separated from irrational assumptions and fears.

4. After challenging your assorted "At Work and School" CMs, use Self-Defense Responses to deal with opponents. In authoritarian relationships in which I've something to gain by staying and choosing to play by the other person's rules, I prefer to use less intimidating counters — NICE NOs and LIMIT-SETTING — whenever possible.

Kay: I have some extra work I'd like you to work on this weekend.

Sarah: Sorry, but I really can't. I've already made plans out-of-town. (NICE NO)

Kay: Too bad. Cancel your plans. I need these files completed by Monday morning.

Sarah: Sorry, but no. I don't feel comfortable canceling my plans. (NICE NO; LIMIT-SETTING)

Kay: I don't care. I order you to cancel your plans.

Sarah: Before we get into a quarrel over this, let's take a couple of minutes to think up some other alternatives. For example, I know Mary is going to be around this weekend. Maybe she'd be willing to cover for me, and then I can cover for her some other time. How about it?

Kay: Well... okay. Let's find Mary. I need to have these files completed.

In this case, Sarah was able to diffuse an escalating power play by keeping calm and rational. By standing her ground, she effectively maneuvered her supervisor into negotiating a workable solution.

Of course, if you decide you've nothing to lose (e.g., if you're going to quit work or withdraw from a class the next week), then go ahead and "pull out all the stops," so to speak.

Carol: You're the most worthless employee I've ever known.

Joe: Hmmm. (READY REPLY)

or

Joe: A stitch in nine saves time. (REVERSE-ORDER READY REPLY)

or

Joe: You seem really hostile. You obviously hate men and have unresolved anger issues. Have you tried getting professional help lately? (PROCESS COMMENT)

or

Joe: (silently glaring) (ICE-COLD GLARE)

Here's another example:

Billy Boss: You're no good. Your work isn't worth the money I pay you.

Jack-Of-All-Trades: Just think, if I were good, you couldn't afford me. And then why would I want to work for you? (SMART ALECK)

And still another:

Student: May I see you for a moment about signing my drop slip?
Professor: I don't have time for people who drop my classes. Why don't you just miss the deadline and lose your tuition? You deserve it for withdrawing from my brilliant class.
Student: Actually yours was the most brilliant course I've ever taken. Unfortunately, my mother's in the hospital, and I have to cut down on my academic load. I sure I hope I can take your class next semester. (FLATTERING)
Professor: I'll sign, no problem. Where's your slip?

or

Professor: I don't have time for people who drop my classes. Why don't you just miss the deadline and lose your tuition? You deserve it for withdrawing from my class.
Student: Will you please repeat what you just said. I want to write down you remarks verbatim so that I quote you correctly when I see the dean in a few minutes. I'm sure he'll be interested to hear what you just had to say to me. You know, I think the school newspaper might also like to hear about it. (PROCESS COMMENT)
Professor: On second thought, where's your slip?

5. Unwanted sexual remarks, touching, etc., are a very real and serious problem in authoritarian situations. Although they usually happen between male bosses or teachers and their female employees or students, there are increasing reports of female bosses harassing male employees, male bosses harassing male employees, etc. Never tolerate sexual harassment from *anyone,* regardless of their position or the threats they make. Instead, immediately report such behavior to the person's supervisor or boss, as well as your own. And depending on the circumstances, you may also want to consider contacting an attorney.

6. Use psychological self-defense strategies to deal with difficult coworkers and classmates, the same as you'd do with any other opponent with whom you're on equal standing. The strategies and techniques you use with difficult relatives and friends also apply to coworkers and classmates.

7. If you feel you're being treated unfairly, complain! First, directly confront your opponent about the situation. Second, take an unresolved case to the highest individual or committee within the particular organization. If, for example, after talking to no avail with a professor who has given you an unfair grade, complain to the professor's chairman, dean, or provost. The same principle applies in the business world.

8. Because of the nature of authoritarian relationships, your options for overcoming a problematic situation may be limited. If you've exhausted all possibilities (including filing complaints), and you're at wit's end, it may be time to move on. In most cases, staying with a sinking ship isn't worth the effect on your nerves or health. If for some reason you can't pack up your office or withdraw from a class, then you'll have to find your answers within yourself.

9. If you feel "lost" career-wise, or if you're just looking for a change, seek out a career counselor or psychologist who can give you vocational interest and aptitude tests. These tests provide valuable information to help you make the most effective decisions possible in terms of a career move. For example, the *Strong-Campbell Interest Inventory (SCII)* and the *Kuder Occupational Interest Survey* (KOIS) measure and compare your reported work interests with those of people already working in various occupations.

Cognitive Reframing Chart
("At Work and School")

Situation:

Crazy-Maker:
Dispute:
Sensible Reply:

Situation:

Crazy-Maker:
Dispute:
Sensible Reply:

Situation:

Crazy-Maker:
Dispute:
Sensible Reply:

Situation:

Crazy-Maker:
Dispute:
Sensible Reply:

Chapter 20

At the Store

We're all born brave, trusting, and greedy,
and most of us remain greedy.
                    — **Mignon McLaughlin**

I hate it. And you probably hate it, too. Dealing with greedy, pushy, and dishonest salespeople. As a friend of mine recently wrote concerning a bad experience buying his first car:

"How exciting it was to walk into that showroom — all those shiny new cars! Before I had a chance to look around much, though, I was met by a very charming, clean-cut gentleman in a suit, whose words were enough to inspire me to take a test drive. We stepped outside, got into one of those 'beauties,' drove around for a few minutes, and then returned. Up to this point, the process was really fun. All he had really asked me was where I worked, how much I wanted to spend, and what size monthly payments I could afford. I had never bought a car before (I was 21 at the time), so I didn't know exactly what to expect.

"You always hear about 'car dealers,' but this guy seemed as far away from being a typical car salesman as you could get. Ha! Was I wrong! Before I knew it (looking back now, though it didn't seem that way at the time), this guy had me wrapped around his little finger. First, he told me he was selling cars at a loss — that day only — to make room for next year's models, which were to arrive at any time. He said the price on the vehicle was what his company had paid for the car (that's how he defined the Manufacturer's Suggested Retail Price,' or MSRP), and that he hated to let *me rip him off*, but that he was going to lose his job if he didn't sell just one more car before the end of the day. Dummy, here, bought all of this hook-line-and-sinker (how was I supposed to know, my first time doing this?). Then he said his manager would be very mad that I was buying such a great car for only the MSRP price, but that he was on my side, and would go and talk to him. Again, he warned me not to get my hopes up too high. So to make me feel better, the salesman offered me a cola to drink while I waited. Looking back, what a nice guy! For the cost of a cola, he got to stick it to me!

"The salesman returned 15 minutes later with the 'unbelievably good news' that he had somehow convinced his manager to let the car go for the MSRP. Naturally, I was elated, as I was led to believe the manager was doing me a big favor! After he ran a credit check (if only I'd had bad credit!) and I agreed to an exorbitant down payment and spendy monthly payments (the dealer did throw in a neat set of designer floor mats at no extra charge), I drove out of the showroom in my brand new car.

"Several months later, I realized what a mistake I had made, and that I'd been taken. It turns out I could have gotten the same model for thousands less, with almost no money down, and much lower monthly payments. At the time I didn't know any better, and I thought I was getting a good deal, so at least I've got a meager excuse. But what about that salesman and his manager? What gave him the right to take advantage of me like that? Where was his sense of decency and integrity? What happened to professional ethics?

"I still feel emotionally violated and angry when I think about it. And I now know this sort of thing goes on all the time. It's enough to make you want to stay home and read books on 'monastic living.' That way you never buy anything, and you avoid having to go out and tangle with all the cheats and thieves." (Nick, age 27; from the Author's files)

My friend Nick's story is a sad but all too common one. If you haven't been there yourself, you probably know of someone who has. We'd be shocked as a society, I'm sure, to discover just how many people are swindled in the car market each year! As my clinic director pointed out to me after I paid too much for my new pickup truck (Yes, Dr. Z. has gotten the stick, too), "When it comes to buying a car, you never win. It's only a matter of how badly you lose."

This taking advantage of innocent buyers isn't limited to car salespeople. It extends into all areas of sales — real estate, appliances, bedding, electronics, musical instruments — almost anything involving the exchange of money. Advantage-taking seems to be an unfortunate byproduct of our society's lucre-focused, "Screw-The-Buyer-At-Any-Cost" mentality.

Certainly, not all salespeople are greedy and unscrupulous. In fact, I've been in retail sales myself, and I know of many fine people in both the wholesale and retail business. So we best not throw out the baby with the bath water — not all salespeople are out to rip you and me off.

My comments in this chapter, then, are directed at helping you defend yourself, not against the good salespeople, but against the bad ones — those who are out to take advantage of you. With this in mind, here are some of Dr. Z.'s practical pointers for protecting yourself in the market place:

1. Be a wise consumer. Know exactly what you want, as well as how much you can afford (and are willing) to pay for it. Resist the temptation to buy on impulse or take on payments you can't afford. My three straight and simple "Don't" rules for being a wise consumer are:

   • *Don't* buy an item you're not fully informed on.
   • *Don't* buy an item you can't afford.

* *Don't* buy an item you don't need, unless you carefully plan for it.

2. Avoid falling victim to sales ploys. Identify and understand the psychology of your sales opponent. Here are four of the nastier types you're likely to encounter:

   a. *The Pressurizer salesperson.* This one turns up the heat to pressure you into buying. For example, he might do his best to convince you that you absolutely *must* buy the RV you're looking at today, because a retired couple from Florida is ready to close on the unit.

   b. *The Squasher salesperson.* The Squasher type will do anything for a sale — lie, cheat, steal, insult you — whatever he believes will do the job. This one has no scruples.

   c. *The Guilterizer salesperson.* This type of salesperson tries to sell you on a product by playing on your feelings of guilt and/or sympathy. He might imply you're not a good parent if your kid doesn't have whatever he's selling, or he might just happen to mention during his pitch that he can barely pay his wife's hospital bills because business has been so bad recently.

   d. *The Egotist salesperson.* The Egotist is so arrogant and cold that you want to purchase his product so he'll like you. And this is just what he hopes you'll do.

3. Avoid impulse buying — the financially ruinous hallmark of our "Buy-Now-And-Pay-For-It-Later" credit card culture. Because store owners want you to spend more than you originally planned, they go out of their way to encourage impulse buying. Thus, the odds are stacked against you as soon as you enter a store or dealership. So psychologically arm yourself before going *anywhere* to buy *anything*. Rid yourself of impulse buying "At the Store" Crazy-Makers (CMs), such as:

   • I *must* buy it now, because I *must* have what I want, when I want it. *I can't tolerate the discomfort* of not having what I want.
   • I *must* buy it now, otherwise it won't be there tomorrow.

- I *must* buy it now, otherwise the salesperson won't like me, and that would be *terrible*.
- I *must* buy it now, otherwise the salesperson won't make a sale and might lose his job, or not be able to pay his bills.

There are a number of other "At the Store" CMs you can work on, too, such as:

- I *should* always believe the salesperson.
- I *have* to be polite to the salesperson, even if I'm being swindled. It'd be *awful* to have a confrontation with the salesperson.
- I *must* feel sorry for the salesperson if he looks sad or unhappy.

Who says you *should*, *have* to, or *must* believe all salespeople, be nice to swindlers, feel sorry for the same, or buy things you don't want or need? Nobody, except maybe the higher-ups in the advertising industry. But who says you're *supposed* to do what they say, anyway?

4. Use Self-Defense Responses (SDRs) to handle difficult salespeople, like those described in #2 above. Here are some READY REPLIES (RRs) and one-liners you can use when you shop:

"Just browsing."
"Not today."
"Forget the double-talk. What's the bottom line?"
"It's not worth that price."
"You must think I'm a pushover!"
"I'll think about it overnight."
"I never buy the same day I look at something."
"I never buy a car until my mechanic does an inspection."
"I have a good friend in the so-and-so business. I'll run your offer by him."
"Don't call me; I'll call you if I decide to buy."
"I don't have time for this."

And last but not least, your three most potent counters are:

"NO!"
"NO!!"
"NO!!!"

Any of a number of SDRs besides RRs are also effective against pushy salespeople, although my favorites are URGENCY-BREAKING, the TAPE LOOP, PROCESS COMMENTS, LIMIT-SETTING, and NEGATING. For example:

Saleswoman Sue: You have to buy this refrigerator today!
Hue: I want to think about it first. (URGENCY-BREAKING)
Saleswoman Sue: I promise, sir, it won't be here tomorrow.
Hue: Like I said, I want to think about it first. (TAPE LOOP)
Saleswoman Sue: You're making a big mistake.
Hue: Maybe so, but I still want to think about it. (TAPE LOOP)

or

Hue: You're a little too pushy for my taste. So I think I'll take my business elsewhere. And by the way, I hear your refrigerators are junk, that they break down all the time. Good-day. (PROCESS COMMENT; LIMIT-SETTING; NEGATING)

5. Keep on the offensive, and don't allow sales opponents to put you on the defensive, which is their usual *modus operandi*. From the moment you walk into the showroom or dealership, make it clear to the seller that you're in charge. You can do this in a number of ways, from using the TAPE LOOP (e.g., "I'm not buying today; just looking") to appearing totally uninterested in the merchandise (e.g., "I'm killing some time in here") to flat out telling him that you won't tolerate any monkey business (e.g., "I know every sales gimmick in the book. Do us both a favor; just stick to the facts"). If the seller tries to pull a fast one on you, bring it to his (and his manager's) attention, and then leave.

6. Never appear anxious or overly interested to buy. To do so is to signal the seller that you're a sitting duck. After you've gathered all the facts, be willing to walk away from a purchase. And then do it! That way, you'll have a chance to mull over the facts and decide if the what-cha-ma-call-it is something you really need or can afford, without the thoughtful input of your salesperson.

7. Also be especially leery of the "Silence Ploy," a technique used by many unscrupulous salespeople. This one is based on the premise

that you, the customer, are more likely to buy an item if the salesman intimidates you with his or her silence. Specifically, at a certain point in the sales pitch, the salesman refuses to speak, hoping you'll feel uncomfortable enough to want to please him by making a purchase. The rule of thumb at this point in the dialogue is that the next person to speak loses, which the salesman is hoping will be you. But don't be intimidated, even if you're the first to speak. You can easily win this one with a PROCESS COMMENT.

Salesman Slippery: That hat looks great on you. How do like it?
Hillary: I think it looks pretty good.
Salesman Slippery: (silent; using the silence ploy)
Hillary: (realizing she's on the receiving end of the silence ploy) It looks like you're trying to pull the old silence ploy on me, aren't you? I know the game. And I never do business with someone who tries to pull that one on me. Here's your hat back. Goodbye. (PROCESS COMMENTS; LIMIT-SETTING)
Salesman Slippery: But wait. I didn't mean...

8. Brush up on the basics of negotiating before purchasing a negotiable item (e.g., a car). I recommend you read Roger Fisher and William Ury's (1981) *Getting to Yes*, which is an excellent guide to this topic.

9. Stay clear of extended warranties. You pay dearly in terms of what you get out of them, and they're nothing but pure profit for the dealer. As my Dad remarked to a salesman who was pressuring him into buying one of these warranties, "You mean you want me to pay to cover your defective product? Maybe you should carry better merchandise. Maybe I should buy better merchandise — somewhere else!" The salesman had nothing to say back.

10. Be careful when trading in your car (or anything else). I've never known anyone to win on a trade, except the dealer. Realize that when you buy an item (e.g., a 2-year-old auto with 20,000 miles), the salesperson always wants you to *pay higher*. But when you

want to trade in the same item (e.g., the same 2-year-old auto with 20,000 miles), he or she wants you to *sell lower*. My brother and his wife recently discovered this "buy low/sell high" principle when purchasing a new sedan and working on a trade with the dealer. When they pointed out this inconsistency to the salesman, his reply to their taking a beating on the trade was a sarcastic, "That's just the way the business works."

11. Complain if you think you've been swindled. First, be aware of your rights as a consumer. For example, some states have "lemon laws" whereby you can return a defective product for a refund, no questions asked. Other states have similar laws whereby you can get out of various "deals" you might have been sweet-talked into, like paying a ridiculous amount of money for a health club membership. Next, try dealing directly with the offending organization. After confronting your swindling salesman, go straight to the top dog in the organization. Finally, contact your local Consumer Protection Agency, Better Business Bureau, or attorney for information on how to register a consumer complaint or file a lawsuit.

COGNITIVE REFRAMING CHART
("At the Store")

Situation:

Crazy-Maker:
Dispute:
Sensible Reply:

Situation:

Crazy-Maker:
Dispute:
Sensible Reply:

Situation:

Crazy-Maker:
Dispute:
Sensible Reply:

Situation:

Crazy-Maker:
Dispute:
Sensible Reply:

Chapter 21

On the Phone

The thoughtless are rarely wordless.
— **Howard W. Newton**

The telephone is a marvelous piece of technology. It uses electricity to carry sound. It allows you to communicate with others almost anywhere in the world. It can be a life-saver in an emergency. And thanks to recent advances in telecommunications, you can carry it in your car or pocket, or connect a machine to it that will answer calls while you're away. Computers can "talk" across phone lines. There are even devices that when attached to your phone tell you the number of the person who's calling, before you ever pick up the receiver.

Sounds like a dream come true, doesn't it? Worldwide communication at your fingertips. All positives, right? Think again! If you have, or have ever had, one of these miracle gadgets, you're certainly familiar with the downside of this technological "dream come true."

Phones, or more precisely *unwelcome phoners,* can be a downright pain in the *neck* (or more precisely, *ear*). They intrude into your life and mental space. They interrupt whatever you're doing. They invade your privacy. And for what? Usually, *absolutely nothing important!* The negatives of having a phone are even more noticeable if you have a listed number and no answering machine. Then you're virtually defenseless and at the phoner's mercy. You never know who might be calling, so you feel pushed into answering every call, which in many cases is a waste of your time.

Here's a typical phone scenario (see if it rings a bell for you — oops, another pun!). You've just come in from an exhausting day at the office. You've worked at full speed all day, and probably answered several dozen phone calls, which always seem to come when you're first walking in, working on a critical file, or trying to take a break or leave. You've never bothered to get an unlisted number or answering machine at home, so you just put up with the phone ringing. You know it's annoying, but you just haven't gotten around to doing anything about your phone situation.

Then as soon as it's most inconvenient (e.g., when you're getting in the shower), what happens? The phone rings. You drop whatever you're doing to answer it. After all, it could be a loved one calling from the hospital or the police station, right? So you answer, only to hear a computer-generated voice trying to sell you property in the middle of the desert. Then you go back to what you were doing, and the phone rings again. This time, it's a long-distance company wanting you to switch over to their service. You get suckered into switching or say NO, hang up, and then attempt once again to finish what you started. Of course, the phone rings a few minutes later, and again you're distracted. This time it's someone wanting you to "answer a few questions" for a national poll. By now you give up, go and put on your "I LOST — THEY WON!" tee-shirt, and forget about showering, trying to eat a hot meal, or watching your favorite television show. And if this evening at home is like most, you can look forward to call after call after call.

If you have a phone, especially a listed number, you know as well as I that the above scenario is no exaggeration. I can't begin to count how many times I've spent entire evenings answering and returning silly, pointless phone calls. Business opportunists. Solicitors. Pollsters. Enthusiasts. Religious zealots. Pranksters. It's obscene! (If it sounds to you like I let myself get hot under the collar about unwelcome phone calls, you're absolutely right! This is one of my pet peeves. And why not? I'm a fallible human being, too!)

So what can be done about unwelcome phone calls? Get rid of the phone? If you do, you'll be all the happier for it. Unfortunately, living without a phone at work or home isn't practical for most people, although I know of some who do. It has become nearly impossible, for example, to conduct business without a phone in our fast-paced, "I-Need-It-Yesterday" society. And on the upside, it's convenient to be able to ring up others when *you choose,* or have a phone available for emergencies. The major point to remember here is that a phone (particularly at home) is a *convenience,* not a *necessity.* Humankind survived and flourished for millennia without telephones.

So does this mean if you own a telephone that you're doomed to give into the gadget? Let it tell you how to spend your time? Let it own you, rather than you own it? By now, you know better. *No, you don't have to give in!,* which brings us back to the purpose of psychological self-defense — regaining control of your life. *And regaining control of your life includes regaining control of your telephone!*

"Simpler said than done!" you claim? I agree. Anything you do that bucks "The System" is sure to raise a few eyebrows, if not directly cause you problems. But a little flack never hurts or stops the assertive individual. I therefore present you with some of the self-defense strategies I've used over the years to deal with unwelcome calls and callers:

1. If at all possible, order an unlisted home phone number. Having an unlisted number stops about 80% of nuisance calls, but only if you take care *never* to give the number out. Regrettably, most banks, utility companies, creditors, schools, magazine publishers, hospitals, insurance carriers, etc. will try to pressure you into giving them your home number. They may even tell you that they won't give it out. Wrong! Once you give out your number, it inevitably goes into the "Big Brother Computer," where anyone can get to it. (How do you think solicitors and pollsters get your name and number in the first place? From computers and mailing lists they buy from these esteemed institutions.)

    So don't give in. It's your phone and your privacy that's at stake. It's okay (and important) to stand your ground. (Just think, what would they do if you didn't own a phone at all?) If the institutions continue to pester you, take your business elsewhere (and be sure to tell them why) or give them an "alternate" number (e.g., office back line).

2. Purchase a telephone answering machine with a "call screening" feature. That way, you can screen whatever calls happen to get through, and immediately pick up or later return the ones you decide are worthwhile. An answering machine also has the advantage of recording important messages while you're away or busy.

3. Identify and dispute the irrational ideas you hold about answering and talking on the telephone. Here are three typical "On the Phone" Crazy-Makers (CMs):

- I *must* answer the phone whenever it rings.
- I *must* talk nice to all callers.
- I *must* return all answering machine messages as quickly as possible.

If you're like 99% of the people in our society, you hold one or more "On the Phone" CMs. But — *who says you must* answer the phone, talk to callers, or promptly return messages? Nobody. These CMs are cultural *demands,* based on irrational assumptions of social etiquette and niceness:

- Society says you *must* answer when spoken to, so you always answer the phone.
- Society says you *must* be nice and talk to everybody, so you talk to all callers.
- Society says you *must* never keep people waiting, so you promptly return all phone calls.

"Society says..." so *"I must...," "I must...," "I must..."* Talk about cultural musturbation!

Now don't get me wrong. There's nothing irrational about *choosing* to answer calls, etc. It's when you do so because you believe you *must* that problems begin. Thus —

- Only answer the phone *if you want to.*
- Only talk to callers *if you want to.*
- Only return phone calls *if you want to.*

4. Cognitive reframing accomplished, use various Self-Defense Responses to counter obnoxious calls and callers. Here are some examples:

Mandy: Hello.
Pollster: Hello. My name is Candy, and I'd like to ask for a few minutes of your time this evening. We the National Pollsters Committee are conducting a nationwide survey to see...
Mandy: I'm sorry, but I'd prefer not to participate. Good luck. (NICE NO)
Pollster: Thank you. Good night.

Or another example:

Dr. Z.: Hello.
Solicitor: Good evening, sir. And congratulations! You're a grand prize winner in our national sweepstakes.
Dr. Z.: Great! What did I win?
Solicitor: A brand new fully loaded red sports car.
Dr. Z.: Great! When will you deliver it?
Solicitor: Well, first, because our company gives prizes away for promotional purposes, we need you to purchase one of our many distinguished products this evening. Only $495 gets you a solid gold watch, and the car. How does that sound to you?
Dr. Z: Tell you what. You deliver the car first, and then I'll buy one of your products. How does that sound to you? (LIMIT SETTING)
Solicitor: Well, that's not the way it works.
Dr. Z.: Then I'm not interested. (hanging up immediately) (BLUNT NO)

Or still another:

Jay: Hello.
Religious Proselytizer: Good evening. My name is Ray. If I could have a moment of your time, sir, I'd like to tell you about my religious organization. We're the only true religion, and for a small donation...
Jay: (says nothing and immediately hangs up) (SILENCE)

And the worst — one of those computer-recorded sales pitches:

Sal: Hello.
Computer: Hello. I'm Al, your friendly computer salesman. Your name has been selected from over 10,000 to participate in... (etc.)
Sal: (saying nothing and *not* hanging up, thus preventing the computer from immediately calling someone else) (SILENCE)

We see from these sample dialogues that you can choose to control your phone conversations. You don't *have* to talk to anybody (especially someone who's disturbing you), you're not *required* to be polite, and you can *hang up* whenever you want. Whether you're dealing with obnoxious callers or computers, it's your phone — and your move.

5. Another type of nuisance phone scenario involves trying to call a person or department, only to reach a "computer menu" or secretary who won't put your call through. While these can be frustrating situations, they're also great opportunities to practice patience, accepting that life doesn't always give you what you want. It's also helpful to remember that your options are limited in these situations, so you won't get down on yourself for not being able to reach a certain person or department.

Contrary to what you might be thinking, none of the techniques presented in this chapter are all that complicated, although they may stretch your present views of "interpersonal telecommunications." With a little rethinking and practice, however, you'll be on your way to regaining control of your telephone — and your life.

COGNITIVE REFRAMING CHART
("On the Phone")

Situation:

Crazy-Maker:
Dispute:
Sensible Reply:

Situation:

Crazy-Maker:
Dispute:
Sensible Reply:

Situation:

Crazy-Maker:
Dispute:
Sensible Reply:

Situation:

Crazy-Maker:
Dispute:
Sensible Reply:

Chapter 22

At the Door

Don't jump on a man unless he's down.
— **Finley Peter Dunne**

Have you ever responded to one of those slick advertisements in the back of popular magazines, like the following examples?

- $25,000 grant. Yours for the asking. Never repay. Free details for SASE. Write: Miracle Money. Box $$$, Wealth, USA. 12345
- Million Dollar secret revealed for the first time. Be filthy rich in only one month. Guaranteed. Call 1-900-GET-RICH.
- Have you lived before? Learn about the true religion of the cosmos. Call 1-900-MY-TRUTH.

If you're like me, you've answered at least one of these ads in your lifetime. There's something about them that piques one's curiosity (probably their promise that you'll get "something for nothing"). And here's what usually happens. First, you come across an offer in a magazine that sounds too good to be true, so you write or call in. Next, you receive another ad in the mail, asking for a "processing fee" or donation to receive the information you requested from the first ad.

If you decide to pay the "processing" fee, you receive (12 weeks later, not 2 weeks like the ad promised) some fairly worthless or outdated information, envelope stuffing scam, or illegal chain letter program.

But that's not all you get for your money! You're soon deluged with literally hundreds of "opportunity seekers" advertisements and catalogs. (Many of these mail-order companies make more money selling names and addresses than selling their products!) Multi-level marketing programs. Pyramid schemes. Work-at-home scams. Get-rich-quick strategies. Psychic healer readings for a nominal fee. Religious materials concerning the end of the world. Catalogs. Brochures. Requests for donations. 1-900 opportunities. Government houses and jeeps for $1. Property for sale in the middle of nowhere. Foundation and grant lists. Scholarship Services. Drop shipment deals. And these are only the tip of the mail-order iceberg. If you don't believe me, try answering one of those seemingly innocent ads yourself and see what happens!

What's the worst part of all of this? Receiving a batch of junk mail every day? Not really. Granted, it's a nuisance, but mail is easily dealt with. You can write "Refused — Return to Sender" on un-opened junk letters and drop them back in the mailbox. You can open and toss what turns out to be garbage. Or you can provide the Post-master General with the names of scam artists and those asking you to participate in illegal chain letters. Doing any of these three things will generally stop a good portion of nuisance mail from coming your way.

No, the worst part is when these folks look up your home phone number and call you at night, or show up on your doorstep in the evening wanting to sell you something — be it investing in a shady business deal or joining a fringe religious group. And if you're like me, you find these inconsiderate, unwelcome knocks at your door (especially after work and on the weekends) to be a real pain. Like phone calls, they intrude, interrupt, and invade.

Fortunately, as is the case with unwelcome phone calls, you can change your thoughts, feelings, and behaviors to defend yourself against doorstep solicitors, salespeople, proselytizers, and pollsters. Remember, when people call or show up at your home unexpectedly, their purpose is to catch you off-guard in the hopes that you'll drop your defenses and give in to their sales pitch. Unwelcome calls and visits are an *offensive* move — a deliberate tactic to convince, control, and manipulate you. With this in mind, below are some of my best tricks for getting rid of this type of opponent:

1. Get a "No Soliciting" "Do Not Disturb" or "No Trespassing" sign and attach it to your door. This will discourage at least some solicitors from knocking. The sign also serves as a warning for those who decide to bother you anyway. After all, they may get a door slammed in their face!

2. If at all possible, rent a Post Office box. Have all of your mail sent there, instead of your home. That way, opportunists will have a much harder time finding you, especially if you also have an unlisted telephone number.

3. Use your cognitive reframing skills to rid yourself of "At the Door" Crazy-Makers (CMs), the four most common of which are:

   - I *have* to answer the door whenever somebody knocks.
   - I *have* to talk to everybody who comes to my door, and listen to whatever it is that they have to say.
   - I *have* to invite into my home anybody who comes to my door.

   "At the Door" CMs are based on the cultural *requirements* that you always *have* to listen to and answer others, be polite to them, and even invite them in. So I ask you (and you knew I would!):

   - Where's the rule that says you *have* to answer the door whenever somebody knocks?
   - Who says you *need* to talk to everybody who comes to your door, and listen to whatever it is that they have to say?
   - Where's the law that says you *must* invite into your home anybody who comes to your door?

   The answer to all of these is, *there isn't any such rule, person, or law!* You don't have to do anything unless you choose, including being polite to inconsiderate doorstep opponents.

   But wait! There's another, even more important Dispute to consider —

   - What's the worst thing that will happen if you don't do all the things you feel you *have* to?

— which touches on the issue of *why* people hold on to "At the Door" CMs (or any other kind). They do so because of the *terribleness*, *horribleness*, and *awfulness* they associate with going against society's *shoulds*, *musts*, *oughts*, *haves*, or *needs*. And most people believe they can't tolerate discomfort at all, not to mention if they should buck "The System," which they're sure will bring about *catastrophe* and *disaster*.

So what's the worst thing that can happen if you go against the rules? You end up with an *inconvenient* or *unfortunate* outcome of some sort. Think about it. Is it really *terrible*, *horrible*, or *awful* to not answer the door, refuse to let strangers into your home, or be impolite to doorstep swindlers? Will going against the crowd really bring about *catastrophe*? Can people really not tolerate *discomfort in any form*? The answer to these three questions is, *No! No!! No!!!* That's why we label irrational assumptions of *demandingness* as *Crazy-Makers*. CMs are pure nonsense, having no basis in reality and serving no useful purpose. Therefore —

- Only answer the door *if you want to*.
- Only talk and listen to solicitors, etc. *if you want to*.
- Only invite solicitors, etc. into your home *if you want to*.

One note of caution, however, concerning this last point. You shouldn't invite strangers into your home. First, they could be dangerous criminals. Second, once in your home (even if legitimate and well-meaning), they can be nearly impossible to be rid of, at least until you cave in to their demands. An opponent in your home (especially one who won't leave) puts you in a weak, defensive, and possibly dangerous position.

4. Use Self-Defense Responses (SDRs) to counter doorstep opponents. Although there are many possible scenarios and responses, I offer a few sample dialogues to give you some ideas for handling unwelcome visits:

Arlene: May I help you?
Salesman: Are you the lady of the house?
Arlene: Who wants to know?

Salesman: My name is Mr. Slick Talker, and I'm with Over-priced Water, Inc. I want you to have one of these beautiful water purifiers installed in your home today. You look like a sensible homemaker who wants the best for her family. And what better gift for your loved ones than clean, uncontaminated water to drink, right? I mean, what kind of mother would you be if you didn't give your children clean water? If you'll invite me in to demonstrate our machine, I have a free gift for you, with no obligation. If you'll be so kind as to move aside, I can...

Arlene: Sorry, I'm not interested. Goodbye. (NICE NO)

or

Arlene: No. (BLUNT NO)

or

Arlene: You seem very pushy. No, you may not come in. I don't need a water purifier. And how dare you accuse me of not giving my children clean water to drink. As a matter of fact, I have a mind to turn you and your company into the Better Business Bureau. (closes door) (PROCESS COMMENT; BLUNT NO; LIMIT-SETTING)

As you see, Arlene has a number of SDRs available to deal with Mr. Slick Talker's various sales ploys. Notice how he tries to make her feel guilty for not giving her children "clean water," which she could do if only she'd buy his machine. Slick also does his best to weasel his way into her home. She in turn uses SDRs to keep control of her situation. But she could just as easily have slammed the door in Slick's face if she wanted to!

Here's another typical scenario:

Steve: Yes?
Religious Proselytizer: Good afternoon, sir. And how are you on this lovely day that the Lord hath made?
Steve: Didn't you see the "No Soliciting" sign on my front door? (PROCESS COMMENT)

Religious Proselytizer: (avoiding Steve's question) My name is Saint Bugaboo, and I'm a member of Religious Zealots for a Fanatical Future. The Lord came to me in a dream last night and told me to knock on your door today. Isn't that something?

Steve: (remaining silent, starring) (SILENCE; STARE)

Religious Proselytizer: Yes, well, I've come to teach you about religious truth. If you'll invite me in, and for a small donation to cover my expenses of coming over, I'm prepared to spend as long as necessary to see that your soul is saved.

Steve: (silent and sneering) (ICE COLD GLARE)

Religious Proselytizer: Come on, sir. It's the Lord's will. You can't argue with the Almighty, can you? And I'm sure there's healing for you today, if you'll just let me in. By the way, I accept all major credit cards.

Steve: Get out of here before I call the police! (LIMIT-SETTING)

The "Never-Let-Them-In" rule is particularly applicable to religious fanatics. These can be some of the most obstinate in terms of remaining in your home until you've converted to their religion. Moreover, be especially leery of proselytizers who request a "doorstep donation" to further their cause. Some of them pull a donation request when they see you want them to leave. They figure you'll do anything to get rid of them, so why not ask you for money? Of course, your donation never makes it to headquarters (if there is one), but the proselytizers will have a grand lunch on you! If the proselytizers (and other opponents) won't leave after one of two prompts, then excuse yourself and call the police.

And one final dialogue:

Mindy: What can I do for you?

Petitioner: Hi! I'm Windy, and I'm collecting signatures to protect small animals from being killed to make moccasins. Would you be willing to sign this petition?

Mindy: No thanks. Good luck with your petition. (NICE NO)

Petitioner: You mean you like to see small animals killed?

Mindy: Like I said, no thanks. (TAPE LOOP)
Petitioner: But you're the only one on your block who hasn't signed. What will your neighbors think?
Mindy: Like I said, no thanks. (TAPE LOOP)
Petitioner: Please, please, please sign. If I get just one more signature, the local animal shelter will give me a free trip to Hawaii. Only you can help me out!
Mindy: (closing door) Goodbye.

This one is a good example of how to turn difficult, annoying encounters into psychological self-defense practice sessions. Mindy could have simply said NO or slammed the door at the beginning, but she chose to practice using the TAPE LOOP on the petitioner. And it worked, even when the petitioner tried pulling the "What-Will-Your-Neighbors-Think?" and "Please-I-Just-Need-One-More-Signature" Guilterizer routines. Bravo, Mindy!

COGNITIVE REFRAMING CHART
("At the Door")

Situation:

Crazy-Maker:
Dispute:
Sensible Reply:

Situation:

Crazy-Maker:
Dispute:
Sensible Reply:

Situation:

Crazy-Maker:
Dispute:
Sensible Reply:

Situation:

Crazy-Maker:
Dispute:
Sensible Reply:

A Final Note

I hope you've found the material in *Don't Let Them Psych You Out!* to be helpful in your search for psychological freedom. Although I can't promise to answer all correspondence, I'd like to hear from you regarding any impact my book has had on your life. I'm also available for seminars, workshops, and other speaking engagements. You may contact me at:

Dr. George Zgourides
c/o Loompanics Unlimited
P.O. Box 1197
Port Townsend, Washington 98368

or

Dr. George Zgourides
Department of Psychology
University of Portland
5000 N. Willamette Blvd.
Portland, Oregon 97203

Appendix A
Self-Defense Responses
(A Glossary of Verbal and
Nonverbal Counters)

I STATEMENT — Verbal statement reflecting your thoughts, feelings, and desires; the opposite of accusing and blaming.

PREFERENCE STATEMENT — Verbal statement reflecting your preferences; the opposite of demanding.

BEHAVIOR STATEMENT — Verbal statement describing observable behaviors.

POSITIVE VERBAL TRACKING — Staying on the topic at hand; the opposite of changing the subject.

POSITIVE VOCAL TRACKING — Saying things in such a way that your true intent and interest come across to the other person.

ENCOURAGING — Using certain words and phrases to prompt the other person to continue talking.

PARAPHRASING — Summarizing the most important points of the other person's message.

DETAILING — Asking for specific details.

REALITY CHECKING — Confirming the accuracy of what has just been heard.

POSITIVE EYE CONTACT — Looking directly, but not staring, at the other person during a conversation.

OPEN BODY POSTURE — Uncrossing your arms and legs to prompt the other person to continue talking.

ENCOURAGING GESTURES — Using head nods and open-handed gestures to prompt the other person to continue talking.

READY REPLIES — Short, vague responses for use when you find yourself going blank.

URGENCY-BREAKING — Invalidating the urgency of your opponent's demands.

NEGATING — Invalidating the importance of your opponent's demands.

PASSING THE BUCK — Passing responsibility along to someone else.

REVERSE-ORDER READY REPLY — A type of READY REPLY in which you reverse the main parts of your proverbs and clichés.

TAPE LOOP — Repeating the same word or sentence over and over again.

NICE NO — Saying NO in a cordial and gentle manner.

BLUNT NO — Saying NO in a direct and to-the-point manner.

LIMIT-SETTING — Saying NO by setting your boundaries and refusing to budge.

ACCEPTING THE MONKEY — Accepting a responsibility.

REFUSING THE MONKEY — Refusing a responsibility.

RETURNING THE MONKEY — Returning a responsibility that you no longer want.

INTERRUPTING (CHANGING THE SUBJECT or NEGATIVE VERBAL TRACKING) — Intentionally leaving the topic at hand; the opposite of POSITIVE VERBAL TRACKING.

NEGATIVE VOCAL TRACKING — Using an unexpected vocal tone to make your point; the opposite of POSITIVE VOCAL TRACKING.

PROCESS COMMENT — Response to what is really being said (i.e., the underlying message behind the actual words chosen.)

CONTENT COMMENT — Response to what is apparently being said (i.e., the particular words used to express an idea).

REFLECTING QUESTION — Repeating back everything your opponent says in the form of a question.

AGREEING — Agreeing with everything your opponent says, irrespective of what you really believe.

DISAGREEING — Disagreeing with everything your opponent says, irrespective of what you really believe.

FLATTERING — Paying your opponent all kinds of compliments, which you may or may not mean or believe.

SMART ALECK — Responding to whatever your opponent says with conceited and pretentiously clever remarks.

SILENCE — Intentionally saying nothing to your opponent.

STARE — Meeting your opponent's comments with a blank, emotionless expression on your face.

ICE-COLD GLARE — Intentionally sneering at your opponent.

CALMING STATEMENT — Carefully chosen word(s) for relaxing yourself both before and during stressful situations.

TIME-OUT — Removing yourself from a volatile situation in order to relax and gather your thoughts.

Appendix B
Finding a Reputable
Mental Health Therapist

If you've benefited from reading ***Don't Let Them Psych You Out!***, but you'd like to work on your defense skills in more depth, you may want to seek out the services of a psychotherapist (i.e., a psychiatrist, psychologist, social worker, or counselor). But please heed my warning: just as all new cars aren't alike, neither are all therapists! You need to be an informed consumer and "test drive" one or more therapists before making any long-term commitments (emotional or financial) to individual or group therapy. To this end, I offer you some suggestions for finding a reputable mental health therapist who will work with you on acquiring and mastering the types of skills and techniques outlined in this book:

1. States regulate certain professional titles, such as "psychologist" and "physician," meaning that to use one or more titles, an individual must be certified or licensed by the state following lengthy academic and professional training and examination. States may not regulate other titles, such as "therapist," meaning that virtually anyone — trained or not — can use these titles. It's to your advantage to find a mental health therapist who's certified or licensed by the state in which he or she practices. *The wise consumer is careful to check out his or her therapist's pro-*

fessional credentials, training, and background before starting therapy. Unfortunately, just because a therapist has a license doesn't mean he or she is reputable, ethical, or competent. Professional licensing, however, does tend to protect the general public from most potential hazards.

2.   The best way to locate a reputable therapist in your area is to obtain a referral from a health care provider, or a listing from a local medical/nursing, psychological, social work, or counseling association. The provider or association can also help you decide which type of therapist (e.g., psychiatrist versus psychologist) is appropriate for you and your problem. Never just look up a name in the phone book and make an appointment!

3.   Understand that there's no such thing as "the single, best therapy" for all people in all circumstances. There are, instead, many different formats of therapy, ranging anywhere from short-term individual work to long-term support groups. Various practitioners also have differing perspectives concerning length of treatment, procedures, etc., which adds to the confusion of trying to find a suitable therapist for a particular problem.

It's my view that the most effective therapy for a variety of everyday problems (like the ones described in **Don't Let Them Psych You Out!**) is cognitive-emotional-behavioral (CEB) therapy. If you want to work on cognitive reframing, assertiveness, and psychological self-defense skills, you can't beat *rational-emotive therapy* (a la Albert Ellis) or *cognitive therapy* (a la Aaron Beck). Two added bonuses of these therapies are their time-limited nature and focus on solutions rather than early childhood conflicts.

4.   During your initial appointment, be sure to ask your therapist about her or his professional qualifications, education, training, years in practice, treatment perspective, and professional associations. She or he should have a graduate degree from an accredited institution, as well as substantial postgraduate training, including direct, personal supervision. Also discuss issues of cost, insurance, projected length of therapy, confidentiality, where to have a complete medical exam performed, and what you should do in an emergency or crisis. You should feel com-

fortable with all aspects of the therapist's approach, etc., including her or his personal style of interacting with you. Leave no stone unturned — always be an *informed consumer!* Whether you're buying a refrigerator or seeking a therapist, get all the facts — up front!

5.   Be sure to question any therapeutic recommendations that sound inappropriate or make you feel uncomfortable. *Under no circumstances should a reputable therapist ever advise you to disrobe (partially or fully) or engage in any sexual activity with her- or himself for any reason, including therapeutic purposes!* Immediately report any such request to the nearest professional licensing board or the police.

Appendix C
Finding a Reputable
Sex Therapist

Central to finding the right therapy for a sexual problem is finding the right sex therapist. But how should you go about this? Pull a name out of the phone book? Respond to a slick advertisement in the paper? Get a referral from a friend or health care provider? Given the potential for therapist-client abuse in the sex therapy profession, I offer you the following suggestions to help you locate a reputable sex therapist who's right for you:

1. If at all possible, first seek therapy from a practitioner whose clinic is affiliated with a medical school, university, college, or hospital. Obtain a list of professional therapists in your area from a local medical/nursing, psychological, counseling, or social work association, or obtain a referral from your health care provider. *Never* simply look up a name under "Sex Therapists" in the phone book and make an appointment. Remember, most states don't regulate or license sex therapists. It's conceivable, then, for a person without any training whatsoever to hang a shingle on an office door and open a sex therapy clinic and practice. And a lot of quacks do just that. *Caveat emptor! — Let the buyer beware!*

2. Though not "sex therapists," *per se,* many state licensed and certified psychiatrists, psychologists, counselors, and social workers treat sexual dysfunctions as part of a larger range of professional activities. One of these providers may be an option for you.

3. You should preferably see a therapist who is nationally certified by the *American Association of Sex Educators, Counselors, and Therapists (AASECT)* and/or a member of one of the national sexuality organizations, like the *Society for Sex Therapy and Research (SSTAR)* and the *Society for the Scientific Study of Sex (SSSS).*

4. During your initial appointment, be sure to ask your therapist about her or his professional qualifications, education, training, years in practice, treatment perspective, and professional associations. She or he should have a graduate degree from an accredited institution, as well as substantial postgraduate training in sex therapy, including direct, personal supervision. Also discuss issues of cost, insurance, projected length of therapy, confidentiality, where to have a complete medical exam performed, and what you should do in an emergency or crisis. You should feel comfortable with all aspects of the therapist's approach, etc., including her or his personal style of interacting with you. Leave no stone unturned — always be an *informed consumer!* Whether you're buying a refrigerator or seeking a therapist, get all the facts — up front!

5. Be sure to question any therapeutic recommendations that sound inappropriate or make you feel uncomfortable. *Under no circumstances should a reputable therapist ever advise you to disrobe (partially or fully) or engage in any sexual activity with her- or himself for any reason, including therapeutic purposes!* Immediately report any such request to the nearest professional licensing board or the police.

Selected
References

Benson, H. (1992). *The Relaxation Response.* NY: Wing Books. (Original work published 1975).

Berne, E. (1964). *Games People Play.* NY: Grove Press.

Bramson, R. (1981). *Coping With Difficult People.* NY: Doubleday.

Branden, N. (1988). "A Vision of Romantic Love." In R. J. Sternberg & M. L. Barnes (Eds.), *The Psychology of Love* (pp. 218-231). New Haven, CT: Yale University Press.

Burns, D. D. (1980). *Feeling Good: The New Mood Therapy.* NY: William Morrow.

Burns, D. D. (1989). *The Feeling Good Handbook.* NY: William Morrow.

Carter, J. (1989). *Nasty People: How to Stop Being Hurt by Them Without Becoming One of Them.* NY: Dorset Press.

Dyer, W. W. (1976). *Your Erroneous Zones.* NY: Avon Books.

Elgin, S. H. (1980). *The Gentle Art of Verbal Self-Defense.* NY: Dorset Press.

Ellis, A. (1962). *Reason and Emotion in Psychotherapy.* Secaucus, NJ: The Citadel Press.

Ellis, A. (1988). *How to Stubbornly Refuse to Make Yourself Miserable About Anything, Yes Anything!* NY: Lyle Stuart.

Ellis, A., & Harper, R. A. (1975). *A New Guide to Rational Living.* North Hollywood, CA: Wilshire Book Company.

Fisher, R., & Ury, W. (1981). *Getting to Yes: Negotiating Agreement Without Giving In.* NY: Penguin Books.

James, M. & Savary, L. (1976). *The Heart of Friendship.* NY: Harper & Row.

Maltz, M. (1960). *Psycho-Cybernetics.* NY: Pocket Books.

Nader, R., & Smith, W. J. (1992). *The Frugal Shopper.* Washington, DC: Center for Study of Responsive Law.

Smith, M. J. (1975). *When I Say No, I Feel Guilty.* NY: Bantam Books.

Warren, R., & Zgourides, G. D. (1991). *Anxiety Disorders: A Rational-Emotive Perspective.* Elmsford, NY: Pergamon Press/Allyn and Bacon.

Warren, R., & Warren, T. (1985). *Tender Talk: A Practical Guide to Intimate Conversations.* Portland, OR: The Portland Press.

YOU WILL ALSO WANT TO READ:

☐ **58072 ASK ME NO QUESTIONS, I'LL TELL YOU NO LIES, How to survive being interviewed, interrogated, questioned, quizzed, sweated, grilled...., by Jack Luger.** How to handle any kind of questioning, including police interrogations, job applications, court testimony, polygraph exams, media interviews and more. Learn how to condition yourself against the tricks interrogators use to make you talk. *1991, 5½ x 8½, 177 pp, soft cover.* $16.95.

☐ **58080 THE PRIVACY POACHERS, How Government and Big Corporations Gather, Use and Sell Information About You, by Tony Lesce.** This book explains how various snoops get their hands on sensitive information about you, such as financial records, medical history, legal records and more. This information is packaged and sold, over and over again, without your consent. Find out what they have on you, and what you can do to protect yourself. *1992, 5½ x 8½, 155 pp, Illustrated, soft cover.* $16.95.

☐ **19079 FIGHTING BACK ON THE JOB, by Victor Santoro.** This book tells how to strike back against a lousy boss, jerk fellow employees, the company spy, and anyone else in the workplace who has ticked you off. If you're getting canned, why not take everyone else with you? How about selling company secrets to the competition? Remember, your boss can only wreck your life, you can wreck his business. *Sold for information purposes only. 1982, 5½ x 8½, 149 pp, Illustrated, soft cover.* $12.00.

☐ **94187 ANARCHIC HARMONY, by William J Murray.** "What I found by turning my back on our society-generated mythology was so found I had to share it — presumptuous or not — because it *indicts the social structure of mankind* and *demands social disobedience*, or living according to our inner, *heroic nature* and *not* according to the intimidation and demands of society's ideology." *1992, 5½ x 8½, 144 pp, soft cover.* $12.95.

••

Loompanics Unlimited
PO Box 1197
Port Townsend, WA 98368

Ps96

Please send me the books I have checked above. I have enclosed $_____ which includes $4.95 for shipping and handling of orders up to $20.00. Please include $1 for each additional $15 in books. Washington residents include 7.9% sales tax.

Name _____

Address_____

City/State/Zip _____

Now accepting Visa and MasterCard. To place a credit card order *only*,
call 1-800-380-2230, 9 am to 4 pm, PST, Monday through Friday.